God & Man
on Wall Street

—The Conscience of Capitalism

Brick Tower Press
Habent Sua Fata Libelli

Brick Tower Press
1230 Park Avenue
New York, New York 10128
Tel: 212-427-7139
bricktower@aol.com • www.BrickTowerPress.com

Library of Congress Cataloging-in-Publication Data
Columbus, Craig
Hendrickson, Mark W.
God and Man on Wall Street
Includes biographical references and footnotes
ISBN 978-1-883283-79-7

1. Columbus, Craig— 2. Business—United States 3. Investments 4. Panic of 2008—
Great Recession

First Printing, August 2012
God and Man on Wall Street
The Conscience of Capitalism

God & Man
on Wall Street

—The Conscience of Capitalism

Craig Columbus
and Mark W. Hendrickson

ACKNOWLEDGMENTS
The authors would like to thank uber-agent Alan Morell and
John T. Colby Jr. of Brick Tower Press for believing in the notion of a
better financial world. We also thank our friend and colleague,
Dr. Jim Dupree, for his valuable insight, and the students of Grove
City College for inspiring us. Finally, we especially thank our families
for their love, patience and support.

Table of Contents

Introduction

Financial markets run on faith:
—faith that what you've been told is true
—faith that your property rights are secure
—faith that something really is what a seller tells you it is
—faith that promises and contracts will be honored and, if necessary, enforced
—faith that you can buy, sell or take delivery of your assets from a custodian when you want to
—faith that prices are being reported accurately
—faith that risk ratings are accurate and financial professionals will honestly explain the risks involved in various investments
—faith that a transaction will ultimately settle between the correct parties

Even more fundamentally, money and banks themselves run on faith. In a fractional reserve banking system, banks and other depositary institutions only maintain a "fraction" of customer deposits in their vaults, lending the majority out to (hopefully) creditworthy borrowers. They rely on depositors' faith that they can access their deposits whenever they want. In point of fact, although the possibility is remote, if all of the bank's customers were to show up on any given day to withdraw their deposits (a "run on the bank"), it would be "game over."

Kelly S. King, the chairman and CEO of the nation's ninth-largest bank, BBB&T Corporation, neatly summarized the nature of our financial system when he stated, "The truth is, we live in a faith-based, confidence-based system."[i]

Throughout the summer and fall of 2008, faith flickered on Wall Street and on Main Street. It was a perplexing and baffling time. Which individuals were truly creditworthy? Which firms were financially sound? Which counterparties were reliable? Who could you trust? What were various assets really worth?

Even the most sophisticated security analysts struggled to analyze complex bank balance sheets full of inflated assumptions about crumbling real estate. In turn, banks refused to lend to each other. Rattled hedge funds pulled their money from certain "prime brokers" for fear that their funds would be frozen. Panicked individuals fled the stock market in droves, many selling at huge losses rather than suffer continued uncertainty. Fearing a total collapse of faith in the banking system, the Federal Deposit Insurance Corporation (FDIC) took the extraordinary measure of raising its guaranteed protection for all interest- and non-interest-bearing bank accounts from $100,000 to $250,000.

Like most Americans, I was disillusioned and disheartened by what I saw from Wall Street—appalled at the greed, dismayed by the arrogance. The difference was that financial services—more specifically, asset management—was *my* industry. For fifteen years, I had been a regular on financial television, analyzing financial markets and economic events. When politicians and the media tried to paint the entire financial industry with the same broad brush of immorality and lack of integrity, it only added to my frustration. That's because during my career I had met and worked closely with hundreds of diligent, ethical financial professionals who played by the rules and were deeply committed stewards. Many aspects of the reported selfish, reckless or illegal behavior didn't fit with the Wall Street I knew.

Those were very difficult days for both investors and many in the financial industry who internalized the stresses of a once-in-a-lifetime (I hope) financial meltdown. During this time, I contracted the shingles, which covered half of my face, and slept sparingly on a couch with CNBC Europe always running in the background to stay on top of overnight developments. Our Phoenix, Arizona firm manages assets on behalf of independent financial advisors and their clients. We were far removed from the esoteric mortgage products at the heart of the financial crisis, but it didn't matter. *Everyone* was in the path of this financial hurricane.

I was very fortunate, though, to be offered a hopeful glimpse of the future just when I needed it the most—one that few financial professionals were afforded. Beginning in the fall of 2009, I also began serving as the chair of the Entrepreneurship Department at Grove City College, one of the nation's leading nondenominational Christian colleges. I remembered once seeing an interview with one of the many first responders who arrived at the scene of the 1995 Oklahoma City terrorist bombing. The man recounted how important it was for him to go home that first night, to get his hands in the dirt of his own backyard, and to plant some simple flowers—a sign of new life and renewal. While my own financial crisis experiences were nowhere near that dramatic or gut-wrenching, working with talented and idealistic students was an opportunity to put my own hands in some welcome soil.

Grove City College is particularly unique and rich soil. The school's rock-ribbed commitment to private-market solutions attracts many market-oriented professors including several scholars from the Austrian school of economic thought. The college's deeply held core values blend faith and freedom (and therefore free markets), forming the distinctive character of the institution.

Credit markets were completely frozen during the financial crisis of 2008, and the financial system ground to a halt. But each spring, 1.5 million young people graduate from American colleges and universities like a steady stream, regardless of GDP figures or the level of the Dow Jones Industrial Average. The next generation of entrepreneurs and financiers focus their gaze on the horizon, for it is all they can control. There is something uplifting and liberating about that perpetually optimistic view. I believe finance can be very purposeful work, providing numerous opportunities to serve something more than one's self. I am heartened that both hope and help are on the way.

Academia also offered a chance for me to regularly reflect, in a special environment conducive to contemplation, on the chain reaction of financial events I had recently witnessed. My Grove City College colleague Dr. Mark Hendrickson and I began an ongoing dialogue about Wall Street reform. Mark, an accomplished Austrian economist, is also a man of keen spiritual insight, having previously authored his own book about the unsung heroes of the Bible. He was looking at Wall Street from the outside in, while I was reexamining it from the inside out.

Mark had no ties to the financial industry. He studied under the tutelage of Hans F. Sennholz, who had earned his doctorate in economics under the preeminent Austrian economist of the 20th century, Ludwig von Mises (1881–1973). Mark's primary concern, as an economist, was in the overall health of the economy.

Our running discussions centered on how to encourage a more transparent, fair, and purposeful financial system. We would inevitably reach the same conclusion despite our differing experiences—that additional regulations, *alone*, would not be sufficient. Both market forces and ethical solutions would also be required. Like the legs of a stool, all three solutions—regulatory, market, and ethical—would be needed to restore confidence in both Wall Street and capitalism itself.

Although finance provides the ability to better manage risk, and therefore offers the capacity to make the world a better and safer place, something went terribly wrong in this regard. Any serious overhaul must begin by acknowledging that reprehensible conduct clearly occurred, and it posed a serious threat to our nation's economic security. In short, Wall Street failed us all.

While the extraordinary interventions of the government and the Federal Reserve have rescued the financial system from the brink of implosion in 2008, it seems that very little has changed among the financial elites. Too-big-to-fail (or too "systemic") institutions and unconstrained credit creation by monetary authorities still dominate the landscape. Recurring scandals, a return to lavish compensation practices, and an economic hangover that continues to disproportionately impact Main Street have caused the public's disillusionment with Wall Street to grow rather than subside.

Many excellent books have been released chronicling the specific events surrounding the Lehman Brothers' bankruptcy and the chaotic days that followed in the fall of 2008. It is a very crowded shelf.

Rather than add to the popular "Whodunit on Wall Street" genre, we wanted to examine the events in impersonal terms for the purpose of identifying and addressing the underlying ethical and moral dimensions. We contend that the financial industry's leadership became apathetic to culture and values—a classic management failure. We try not to assign blame to specific financial firms or bankers, though, and use examples only to demonstrate prevalent industry conduct. Our focus is on Wall Street's interpersonal relations. In fact, many of Wall Street's failings are symptoms of larger American problems. How can we treat each other better within the financial system and thus prosper as a nation?

Most of the approaches to financial reform focus on making the financial system "less bad." What if, however, Wall Street could be made "better" by awakening its goodness? Accountability is about more than simply assigning blame. It is also about offering hope.

We therefore thought it was important to do more than paint a superficial caricature of Wall Street, one that sees financial professionals as nothing more than modern-day robber barons and regulators as "asleep at the switch." Neither popular portrayal is accurate.

Several publishers told us that readers would reject a book that also acknowledges the good Wall Street has done and is capable of doing again, and that we should focus exclusively on the briskly selling financial scandal genre. We respectfully disagree.

As it says in the Book of Ecclesiastes, "For everything there is a season."[ii] Federal intervention might have restored the solvency of Wall Street, but it is powerless to restore its soul. No amount of legislation and regulation, however necessary, is sufficient to instill the ethos of trustworthiness, honor and service that alone can rebuild the reputation and legitimacy of Wall Street.

While Wall Street has become incredibly complex, too opaque in some respects, the roots of the epic financial ills are clear. Unconstrained behavior and borrowing have profoundly negative consequences—yesterday, today, and tomorrow.

As painful as the dislocations and damages were, exposing Wall Street's tainted underbelly offers the world a unique opportunity for a profound and desperately needed transformation—an ethical, if not moral, awakening. There are undeniably desolate periods of behavior as human liberty is subject to both virtuous and immoral expression. But they are just that—periods that are episodic in nature. The call-response rhythm has always provided man a pathway for repair.

The goal: reframe the discussion and shift it to the timeless economic truths and ethical principles that Wall Street needs to reaffirm, restore and uphold if it is to regain public trust. Wall Street needs to do this not only for itself, but in order to preserve and strengthen the irreplaceable role that private financial markets play in contributing to human well-being and upon which the future of our country depends.

Craig Columbus
May 2012

Notes
i Kelly King interview with CNBC Television, December 16, 2011, http://video.cnbc.com/gallery?video=3000062811.
ii The Holy Bible: Ecclesiastes 3:1 (New International Version)

1 A Remodel

Americans don't trust Wall Street anymore. It's unlikely they ever fully did. In recent years, however, the term "Wall Street" has come to embody something much darker than periodic scandals and much larger than the financial district in lower Manhattan. For a growing number of citizens, the term now signifies a predatory economic system that deliberately and maliciously institutionalizes income inequality and economic injustice.

In response to the crisis of trust, financial firms are rushing to roll out client-centric mission statements, sprinkled with words like "steward" and "service." They are also investing in ethics training classes that teach broad principles of moral philosophy and hiring armies of expert consultants.

Those are welcome developments, but they have to function as more than marketing strategies. How can we ensure that those values are absorbed into Wall Street's bloodstream and more deeply penetrate its soul—or, said differently, that these values are lived rather than simply pledged?

There is a long way to go in this regard. Greg Smith, a mid-level Goldman Sachs vice president, publicly resigned from the firm in a controversial *New York Times* opinion column that immediately touched off a firestorm of controversy.[i] Smith, who had joined Goldman upon his graduation from Stanford, cited "the decline in the firm's moral fiber" as his reason for leaving after twelve years of service.[ii] It was later reported that Smith allegedly received a $1.5 million advance from a publisher to write a book about his Goldman experiences.[iii]

Has the industry fundamentally changed in recent years? Were the values of Wall Street's by-gone partnership model of a higher ethical tenor? Or has Wall Street been cynical and unscrupulous ever since the founding of the New York Stock Exchange, with this dark underside finally being more fully exposed by a critical blogosphere and a 24-hour news cycle?

It's true that Wall Street has broken the hearts of the investing public many times over the last twenty-five years. There have been jarring panics and collapses, such as the 1987 "Black Monday" crash, Long Term Capital Management, the Russian debt crisis, and the dot-com tech bubble. There have also been numerous ethical scandals involving Kidder Peabody, Drexel Burnham Lambert, Salomon Brothers and MF Global to name just a few.

Populist backlash against Wall Street and its shadowy speculators is nothing new, either. After all, this is an industry that experienced its first crash in 1792! Thomas Jefferson condemned Wall Street's traders as counterrevolutionary "torries (sic),"[iv] and a bomb destroyed J.P. Morgan's Wall Street offices, killing 38 and injuring 400, in a largely forgotten 1920 anti-capitalist terrorist attack.[v]

However, when Lehman Brothers, a firm founded in 1850, unraveled one weekend in September 2008, it was clear that this time was different. Three of the five largest and most venerable investment banks disappeared with stunning speed, gone forever as proud independent entities. When credit markets froze completely, it threatened to sink the entire economy stretching all the way to Main Street. This was a game-changer, and in the public's mind, Wall Street was the match that lit the fuse.

Inspecting the Damage

Market technicians carefully study divergences, or instances where the price of an asset and a related indicator move in opposite directions. In the trust barometer, the diverging numbers should keep Wall Street bosses awake at night. Even after a historic, multi-year, 100 percent–plus rally in US stock prices off their March 2009 bottom and a barrage of expensive Wall Street public relations campaigns to regain customer trust, only 17 percent of respondents had a positive impression of the financial services industry in a 2012 Harris Interactive poll, besting only government and the tobacco industry in terms of popularity.[vi]

With all the negativism, it's not surprising that retail participation in the equity markets has dropped dramatically in the wake of the 2008 financial crisis. One need look no further than a Prudential Financial survey where 58 percent of people claimed to have lost all faith in stocks and 62 percent couldn't name a single firm they trusted.[vii] Mom and Dad walked away from the stock market and have largely remained on the sidelines ever since, preferring to park $3.5 trillion in cash yielding essentially zero.[viii]

With that apprehension came the rise of phrases like "casino capitalism," descriptive of an era of extreme asset price volatility and rampant speculation. Truthfully, few railed against these same excesses when their home prices were spiking preternaturally higher in value earlier in the decade. But with the onset of retirement approaching for many Americans, the investing roller coaster was simply too much for many to stomach.

This fear and anxiety sadly manifests itself in more than Dow points. A study from the Centers for Disease Control and Prevention found that suicide rates rose in eleven of the thirteen recessions occurring between 1928 and 2007.[ix] US suicides rates soared to an all-time high during the Great Depression of the 1930's, with 22.1 suicides per 100,000 individuals.[x] Neither unemployment rates nor suicide rates have risen to Great Depression–era rates during the current "Great Recession," but the US suicide rate has increased every year from the peak of the housing bubble in 2006 through 2009, the last year for which statistics are available.[xi]

A June 2011 Newsweek/Daily Beast poll also revealed that significant scars remained. Seventy percent of Americans said they were nervous about their retirement with 56 percent claiming to have lost sleep over their financial affairs and 26 percent reporting an impact upon their marriage.[xii]

Many of the same economic grievances quickly ricocheted around the globe, touching off a wave of activism. In the fall of 2011, a fledgling protest movement called Occupy Wall Street sprang up in lower Manhattan's Zuccotti Park. It started with a tweet condemning "corporate rule" and eventually spread to "occupations" in 1,600 cities. Some of the movement's core saw themselves as proud successors to the anti-globalization movement or even the Arab Spring demonstrations.

Others wanted to express their feelings of alienation from a lobbyist-dominated political system that enabled bank bailouts and protected financial elites. For disillusioned twenty-somethings, the movement provided a platform to vent over limited job prospects and crushing student loan burdens.

The Occupy Wall Street movement tapped into something very visceral. Paul Taylor of the Pew Research Center put his finger on it: "The Occupy Wall Street movement kind of crystallized the issue: 1 versus 99. [It's] arguably the most successful slogan since 'Hell no, we won't go,' going back to the Vietnam era."[xiii] In the movement's early days, almost half of the public thought the sentiments at the root of the sometimes incoherent movement generally reflected the views of most Americans.[xiv] Forty-seven percent of Americans also said that Wall Street hurts the US economy more than it helps.[xv] Politicians, reading the same polls, stepped up their own rhetoric and regulatory pressure on Wall Street.

Flooding in the Basement

Not only was the scope of the 2008 financial meltdown different, but so was its depth. The pain went beyond Wall Street and shook the moorings of capitalism itself. Peruvian essayist and Nobel Prize winner Mario Vargas Llosa observed that this financial crisis has "done the most harm to morality."[xvi] Saying the crisis revealed "an essential lack of ethical values and an egocentric spirit," Vargas Llosa warned, "This is the most serious aspect of the crisis and the one that will surely take the longest to remedy."[xvii] Senator John Kerry (D-Massachusetts) even suggested Wall Street's practices revealed a "lack of patriotism," telling radio talk show host Don Imus, "It's just, 'Hey, let's just make our money and run. Devil be damned what the implications are.'"[xviii]

The reputational harm jumps out of the domestic polling data, even well into the modest, post-meltdown economic recovery. Forty percent of Americans have a negative reaction to the term "capitalism" according to a December 2011 Pew Research Center poll.[xix] Even more disturbing, a majority of Americans ages 18-29 actually viewed socialism more positively than capitalism.[xx]

The financial crisis also damaged capitalism's standing in the world – squandering a unique opportunity to slam the door shut on failed economic alternatives. After the demise of the Soviet Union in 1991, the number of people living in market-based economies swelled to record levels and socialism appeared to be in its final throes. However, the painful global economic dislocations of the last few years contributed, at least in some part, to the rise of leftward-leaning presidents in Brazil, Argentina, Uruguay, Chile, Bolivia, Ecuador, Guatemala and Nicaragua. It's not surprising to see the reemergence of statist arguments for more government activism, given the human damage of the "Great Recession."

Mr. Vargas Llosa explained, "Precisely when its most dangerous adversary, communism, was fading, defeated by its internal contradictions and failings, the capitalist system, instead of garnering strength from recent historical evidence that it was the best system to guarantee the holy trinity that Hayek defined as the driver of civilization—property, law and freedom—also began to decay, the victim of a poison its immune system had allowed to flourish instead of attacking and eradicating it."[xxi]

A Remodel, Not a Teardown

Some of the criticism of Wall Street has been a pretext for politicians to advance a wealth redistribution agenda. Other charges have been leveled by disgruntled insiders with personal axes to grind. Much of the criticism, however, has been completely justified. There is simply no excuse or justification for the industry's self-indulgent behavior.

There is a great danger, though, in completely rejecting capitalism, for the simple fact that there is nothing better with which to replace it. With no viable alternative, constructive reform of the existing financial system is, therefore, the only option.

Each of the alternative economic models has proven to be both ineffective and even more prone to corruption and abuse! For example, socialism's inadequacies were fully exposed long ago. In 1891, for example, Pope Leo XIII wrote in his encyclical, *Rerum Novarum: On the*

Condition of the Working Classes, that the "fundamental principle of Socialism, which would make all possessions public property, is to be utterly rejected because it injures the very ones whom it seeks to help."[xxii] China's export-driven state capitalism, fueled by massive reserve accumulation to prevent its own currency's appreciation, is struggling with artificial imbalances, overcapacity, and growing civil tension. The same can be said of Europe's quasi-capitalist public pension model. European Central Bank President Mario Draghi acknowledged the failure: "You know there was a time when [economist] Rudi Dornbusch used to say that the Europeans are so rich they can afford to pay everybody for not working. That's gone."[xxiii] Herman de Rompuy, president of the European Union, bluntly conceded, "We can't finance our social model anymore."[xxiv]

Given the manifest flaws in alternatives to capitalism, many authors and commentators have recognized that it is vital that capitalism's good name be restored. That is not enough, however. Two other closely related terms must also be vindicated: capital and capitalist. There is no capitalism without capital and capitalists.

In its fundamental economic sense, capital is simply one of the factors of production, along with land (natural resources) and labor, which the entrepreneurial or managerial mind uses and arranges to produce goods or services. "Capital" is a value-free word. It is no more "good" or "evil" than nouns like "rock" or "river."

Whether we are talking about financial capital or the capital goods into which financial capital is translated, capital comes from savings. It is income or wealth that exists now as the product of earlier economic activity. But instead of being consumed in the present, it is saved and employed toward the production of goods and services that will be consumed at some future time. The classic example of this is the proverbial seed corn—the part of this year's harvest that a farmer will refrain from consuming this year so that he may use it to plant next year's crop.

Every society, without exception, needs capital in order to survive and prosper. "A country becomes more prosperous in proportion to the rise in the invested capital per capita."[xxv] Without capital at their disposal, workers' productivity is very low and poverty prevails. The historical record shows that wages and standards of living rise as the result of increases in the productivity of labor, and in turn, the primary reason for higher productivity of labor is how much capital labor has at its disposal.[xxvi] A ditch-digger who uses a backhoe not only moves more dirt per hour and consequently receives more pay, but is freed from the back-breaking exertions that a worker equipped only with a shovel must endure.

Finance can therefore serve as a powerful force for good by helping to make available the capital that lifts people out of poverty through enhanced productivity. Countries that have the highest capital per capita invested are the countries where the standards of living are highest or whose economies are growing at the fastest rates. Even China's Communist Party leaders are decidedly pro-capital.

Unfortunately, the quality and effectiveness of capital have been complicated by our fiat money system. Central banks have the ability to create the illusion that there is more capital available than what actually exists, fashioning a false sense of security to monetary policy solutions. Central banks can conjure fiat money and credit out of thin air and so create "counterfeit capital" that competes in the marketplace alongside genuine capital—the savings of thrifty people—to bid for the finite supply of real goods and services. Real capital, however, is wealth that first has to be produced so that it can then be saved and invested. You can't "invest" something that hasn't been produced and doesn't even exist!

Counterfeit capital is, therefore, illusory and dishonest. It redistributes existing wealth to favored institutions and the people who populate those institutions. It inflates bubbles and shifts economic production away from what the public values most highly to politically favored businesses via subsidies, bailouts, etc.—a practice justly derided as "crony capitalism," a.k.a. "corporate capitalism." It is "crony capital" that breathes life into "crony capitalism."

The abundance of capital has also changed the function and identity of today's capitalists. Historically, capitalists were the entrepreneurs who used capital to supply capital goods for workers to use in the production of goods or services that consumers wanted. Today, there is so much capital (both real and fiat) in the world that when we use the term "capitalist," it seems best suited to a professional class of specialists, the financial experts of Wall Street. These are today's purest capitalists, whose primary work is managing capital.

Wall Street (and its global counterparts) now provides more financial options than ever before. Today, capital is potentially available to virtually anyone with a good business plan. Unknown, would-be entrepreneurs have more opportunities to obtain funding than ever before. Large market capitalization corporations can develop in just twenty years' time (think Google and Facebook). The vast network of financial institutions and services is the arena of vigorous competition to find and finance the next new products, services and innovations. Thus the democratization of capital (real capital, that is) is a very powerful and positive force; the unchecked proliferation of fiat capital is not.

Wall Street occupies a crucial—in fact, indispensable position in our economy: that of gatekeeper to the flow of capital. Capital is the lifeblood of the economy. It needs to circulate healthily to where it can accomplish the most good and create the most wealth. Financial professionals are the experts, the doctors of the "blood and circulatory system" upon whose skill we all depend for a productive, well-functioning economy. The financial system routes and "rents" investment capital to those who need it.

This crucial role places an awesome responsibility on the shoulders of Wall Street. The "capital doctors" deserve to be handsomely compensated when they perform their vital functions well and with honor. Just as we would find it natural for heart specialists to be well compensated for using their specialized skills to keep patients alive, so few people will object when Wall Street capitalists use their specialized skills to keep the economy humming on all cylinders.

What has angered so many Americans in the last few years is the perception that Wall Street has continued to get richer while the overall economy has languished. If money or capital is the lifeblood of the economy, then Wall Street has become, in the eyes of many, a vampire, siphoning precious blood-capital from the economy to enrich itself at the expense of everyone else. This, then, defines the challenge facing today's capitalists, the financial pros in the extensive Wall Street universe: either succeed in deploying capital in a way that increases general prosperity, or forever ruin the reputation of "capitalists" and run the risk of a backlash that leads to personal condemnation, and also to the death of the goose that lays the golden egg of affluence—capitalism itself.

The term "crony capitalism" is a demagogic tactic, a distortion. "Crony capitalism" (and this is true of "corporate capitalism," too) is not a form or variation of capitalism, but rather a rejection of it. Wall Street is not the enemy of the American people but rather an important benefactor—*if* its ethical lapses can be curbed. In his historical analysis, *Wall Street: America's Dream Palace*, author Steve Fraser explains, "Lodged deep within our collective psyche these contending incongruent images of Wall Street illuminate its paradoxical history in American culture, suggesting that Main Street and Wall Street have found themselves in a strange love-hate codependency for a very long time."[xxvii]

America needs Wall Street again, albeit with a new operating system installed. Given the forces of globalization and demographic aging, the nation needs a sound financial sector for both entrepreneurial competitiveness and retirement security. A restoration of the industry's proud traditions is therefore required—including patriotism, enlightened self-interest and service to others.

Perhaps Warren Buffet explained it best when he said Wall Street "does a lot of good things and then it has this casino."[xxviii] "It's like a church that's running raffles on the weekend,"[xxix] Buffet told a conference audience in 2010. Wall Street reform is, in fact, a remodel of its social hall rather than a teardown of Mr. Buffet's entire church. Like any good appeal to remodel the church social hall, moral capitalism requires a respectful dialog among the entire congregation—and then lots of hard work to set the world to right.

Notes, Chapter 1

i Greg Smith, "Why I am Leaving Goldman Sachs", *The New York Times*, March 14, 2012.
http://www.nytimes.com/2012/03/14/opinion/why-i-am-leaving-goldman-sachs.html?_r=1&pagewanted=all

ii Ibid.

iii Christine Kearney, "Former Goldman exec Smith lands lucrative book deal: report," *Reuters*, March 30, 2012.
http://uk.reuters.com/article/2012/03/30/goldman-smith-book-idUKL3E8EU70Z20120330.

iv Steve Fraser, *Wall Street, America's Dream Palace* (New Haven: Yale University Press, 2008), 4.

v Paul Kengor, "In 1920, US saw the carnage of class warfare", *USA Today*, November 8, 2011.
http://www.usatoday.com/news/opinion/forum/story/2011-11-08/occupy-wall-street-bombing/51125358/1.

vi Kevin Roose, "Wall Street's Reputation Still Falling", *The New York Times DealBook*, February 13, 2012.
http://dealbook.nytimes.com/2012/02/13/wall-streets-reputation-still-falling/.

vii Walter Hamilton, "New stock market formula: Recession + losses = extreme fear", *Los Angeles Times*, June 1, 2011.
http://latimesblogs.latimes.com/money_co/2011/06/new-stock-market-formula-recession-losses-extreme-fear.html.

viii John Waggoner, "Reserve Primary money market fund breaks a buck," *USA Today*, September 17, 2008.
http://www.usatoday.com/money/perfi/basics/2008-09-16-damage_N.htm.

ix Sara Murray, "Suicide Rates Spike During Recessions", *The Wall Street Journal* Real Time Economics Blog , April 18, 2011.
http://blogs.wsj.com/economics/2011/04/18/suicide-rates-spike-during-recessions/.

x Ibid.

xi American Foundation for Suicide Prevention,
www.afsp.org/index.cfm?page_id=04ea1254-bd31-1fa3-

c549d77e6ca6aa37<http://www.afsp.org/index.cfm?page_id=04ea
1254-bd31-1fa3-c549d77e6ca6aa37>.

xii Douglas Schoen, "America the Angry," *The Daily Beast*, June 4,
2011. http://www.thedailybeast.com/articles/2011/06/04/anger-in-
america-could-the-arab-spring-happen-in-the-us.html.

xiii Scott Horsley, "The Income Gap: Unfair or Are We just Jealous,"
NPR, January 14, 2012.
http://www.npr.org/2012/01/14/145213421/the-income-gap-
unfair-or-are-we-just-jealous.

xiv "Public Opinion and the Occupy Movement," *The New York
Times*, November 9, 2011.
http://www.nytimes.com/interactive/2011/11/09/us/ows-
grid.html.

xv Andrew Kohut, "Haves and Have-Nots", *The New York Times*,
October 27, 2011.
http://www.nytimes.com/roomfordebate/2011/10/18/the-
psychology-of-occupy-wall-street/occupy-wall-streets-taps-into-
longstanding-concerns.

xvi Mario Vargas Llosa, Speech to the Atlas Liberty Forum and
Freedom Dinner, November 9, 2011.
http://atlasnetwork.org/blog/2011/11/capitalism-liberty-and-
morality/.

xvii Ibid.

xviii "Kerry: Wall Street Has 'Lack of Patriotism,'" *Fox Nation*, April
28, 2010. http://nation.foxnews.com/financial-
overhaul/2010/04/28/kerry-wall-street-has-lack-patriotism.

xix Nicholas D. Kristof, "Is Banking Bad?," *The New York Times*,
January 18, 2012.
http://www.nytimes.com/2012/01/19/opinion/kristof-is-banking-
bad.html.

xx Ibid.

xxi Vargas Llosa, Speech to the Atlas Liberty Forum.

xxii Tom Bethell, *The Noblest Triumph: Property and Prosperity Through
the Ages* (New York: St. Martin's Press, 1998), 10.

xxiii Brian Blackstone, Matthew Karnitschnig, and Robert Thomson,
"Europe's Banker Talks Tough", *The Wall Street Journal*, February

24, 2012. http://online.wsj.com/documents/print/WSJ_-A001-20120224.pdf.

xxiv Aoife White, "Trillion-dollar euro rescue won't solve low growth," *The Associated Press*, May 10, 2010. Aoife White, "Trillion-dollar euro rescue won't solve low growth," *The Associated Press*, May 10, 2010.

xxv Ludwig von Mises, *Economic Policy* (South Bend: Regnery/Gateway, Inc., 1979), 14.

xxvi F.A. Harper, *Why Wages Rise* (Irvington, NY: The Foundation for Economic Education, Inc., 1957), 14-34.

xxvii Fraser, *Wall Street, America's Dream Palace*, 3.

xxviii Andrew Frye and Natalie Doss, "Buffet Compares Wall Street to Church with Raffle", *Bloomberg*, October 5, 2010. http://www.bloomberg.com/news/2010-10-05/buffett-compares-wall-street-casino-culture-to-church-raffles.html.

xxix Ibid.

2 Blueprints

Wall Street is capable of goodness. This seems like an absurd statement given all the recent evidence to the contrary. The financial industry's reputation has suffered a devastating body blow. *Wall Street Journal* columnist and former presidential speech writer Peggy Noonan asked, "Noble. Constructive. Admirable. When was the last time anyone thought of Wall Street like that?"[i]

The reality is that many who work in the financial world think of the work they do *exactly* in those terms. These men and women are not delusional nor in denial. Rather, they are simply shaped by their own workaday experiences, their own close personal relationships with colleagues, customers and clients. They are proud to be financial professionals and view their *own* work as both essential and ethical. A telling number of sons and daughters also seem to follow in the same financial career path as their parents. They carry on a family tradition with as much pride as second- and third-generation firefighters and police officers.

Referring to Wall Street's current unpopularity, former treasury secretary and Wall Street veteran Henry "Hank" Paulson, Jr. lamented, "It's so, so sad because I believe banking is and should be a noble profession."[ii] The financial profession can be honorable, even if some recent conduct clearly was not. In fact, some within the industry have been among Wall Street's harshest and most informed self-critics—deeply frustrated at those in the financial community who have sullied capitalism's good name.

Yet, many on Wall Street feel that Washington unfairly demonizes the financial industry for political gain. "I think the basic problem is the president has hurt their feelings," Representative Barney

Frank, the longtime chairman of the House Financial Services Committee, said of the industry in 2011 interview.[iii] People, Frank explained, "want to be told that what they do is not only profitable but socially valuable. That they're good people. And I've tried not to demonize people. That's easy to do. Very few of them are bad people."[iv]

Noted Yale economist Robert Shiller told his undergraduate economics students during the worst days of the financial crisis that he too believed the industry's tarnished reputation was, in many ways, undeserved.[v] Of course, Shiller said, human beings can behave badly, and some people get self-important when they make a lot of money.[vi] Then, invoking our common humanity, Shiller stated, " . . . that there is a moral dilemma underlying all of our economic lives and I think this moral dilemma is the same as the moral dilemma in finance."[vii]

Former George W. Bush speechwriter William McGurn ventured, "When the money is too cheap and fast, it promotes excess. You don't have that spectacle in a college professor, not because he is more moral, but because he doesn't have quite the income."[viii] Corruption, in all its forms, is a very large "industry," with the estimated annual level of worldwide bribery between firms and the public sector exceeding $1 trillion.[ix] This figure does not even include embezzlement of public funds or the theft of public assets.[x] In the words of author and philosopher Michael Novak, "There is nothing human that can't be corrupted."[xi]

Create and Redeem

Unlike other debased areas of global society, however, Wall Street has a unique opportunity to address its corrupt practices and moral failures. The financial crisis of 2008 laid bare many of the financial system's shortcomings, bringing them up to the surface and exposing them to the light of day. It's all out in the open now.

Ethicist Dr. David Gill of Gordon-Conwell Theological Seminary says God is constantly calling man, just as David was called from the fields,[xii] into areas of the world most in need.[xiii] The word "vocation" itself comes from the Latin root "to call." Gill hypothesizes that human beings bring their "best self" to work when offered abundant opportunities to create and redeem, i.e., to fix something or heal harm.[xiv]

When seen in these terms, Wall Street has much to offer a new crop of young professionals eager to make a difference. Young people are increasingly attracted to situations that allow them to register an immediate impact. Think of the response of young Americans to Hurricane Katrina. Many of them played a critical role in rebuilding both the infrastructure and quality of life of hurricane-ravaged New Orleans. They answered the call.

Wall Street, at this moment in time, with its technological horsepower, its highly-skilled innovative workforce, and its abundant chances to heal a variety of existing wrongs, allows participants to create and redeem like never before! Dr. Gill's ideal conditions exist. They won't usher in a renewal, however, if the industry continues to incentivize reckless conduct or subordinate client interests.

The financial sector remained the most popular career for all Harvard graduates in 2011, for example, with 17 percent of the class finding full-time Wall Street work.[xv] Many students are drawn not only to the financial rewards, but also to the industry's extensive training programs which develop highly portable financial literacy and valuation skills.[xvi]

The financial industry may be able to reel in the best and brightest recent graduates with outsized compensation packages and advanced training, but it won't be able to keep them or develop a new leadership tier on that basis alone. In order to retain the leaders of the next generation, Wall Street must genuinely commit to a new values-centric ethos.

The CEO of video game maker Electronic Arts, John Riccitiello, summarized the attitudes of Generation "X" and "Y" workers: "My generation did what they were told, by and large, in business. The generations that followed the baby boom in one flavor or another needed to believe before they could act, and I think I've got to sell them. But you can't sell a skeptic."[xvii] In the words of Jeremy Foster, a Yale MBA student, "Young people today see business differently. They want to know how their values play out in their career."[xviii]

With the growing emphasis on ethics-infused business education, a significant cross-section of students believe they can function as the vanguard of reform in a variety of industries. Business school graduates no longer view for-profit or nonprofit careers as an either-or choice. "The boundaries between the sectors are getting increasingly blurry," says Laura Moon, director of Harvard Business School's Social Enterprise Initiative.[xix] Because more than two-thirds of MBAs graduate with over $40,000 in student loan debt (as of 2008, the latest available data), many students seek for-profit jobs that also address society's important needs.[xx]

Create

The financial world has much to offer in this regard. Finance's continuous cycle of innovation has historically produced significantly more good than harm for the broader economy and is capable of doing so again. Unfortunately, that was clearly not the case with many crisis-era innovations that focused on commission-generating, leverage-dependent products. Exotic mortgage derivatives, for instance, generally lacked logic or redeeming value. We address this issue in detail later, but just as junk science invalidates the scientist who practices it rather than the need for scientific inquiry, the same is true of financial engineering. Evaluating failed innovations, Yale's Dr. Shiller said, "I think that we should be very careful not to let that deflect us from the recognition that this is important technology and that it's not the technology that's at fault; we have to get it right and then it will be powerful."[xxi] Forbes contributor Arjan Schütte echoed similar sentiment: "While clearly much of the financial industry should not be allowed to play with matches, it is a mistake to rule out financial innovation that can be lasting, positive and scalable. In fact, it's highly necessary."[xxii]

Designing appropriate risk management mechanisms is part of the self-healing nature of market capitalism's innovation ecosystem. Even one of the harshest critics of financial innovation run amok, Nobel Prize-winning economist Joseph Stiglitz, acknowledged this potential: "By reducing risks faced by individuals and firms, e.g., through insurance products, a good financial system contributes to greater security and societal well-being, in ways that may not even be fully reflected in GDP statistics."[xxiii] Done properly, finance's risk management function erects an important safety net under society.

It's also important to remember how truly pervasive financial products are in daily life. The financial services cluster consists of four major sub-clusters:[xxiv]

1. **Banking and Credit Intermediation**: including commercial banks, savings institutions, credit unions, credit card issuing, consumer lending and mortgage financing
2. **Securities Dealing and Brokerage**: including investment banking, securities and commodities brokerage, securities and commodities exchanges, portfolio management and investment advice
3. **Insurance**: including life, health, property and casualty insurance, reinsurance, claims adjusting and title insurance
4. **Funds, Trusts and Other Financial Vehicles**: including pension funds, private equity, hedge funds and venture capital

Financial innovation takes the form of better analysis techniques, data mining software, and compliance tools, to name just a few. It is also represented by new instruments that better suit specific customer needs. Some of these instruments are readily accessible to individual savers and investors, like low-fee exchange-traded and index funds, online discount trading and banking, and equity-indexed insurance and annuity products. We take many of these seemingly common financial instruments for granted, yet the first fixed-rate time certificate of deposit (CD) was not introduced until 1961.[xxv] Individual investors have also been armed with a plethora of real-time online research and information products, tools that were previously only in the hands of professional traders.

Other innovations, such as sophisticated hedging techniques for a corporation's fluctuating commodity costs, or enhanced settlement techniques for electronic transactions, go on largely beyond the public's view. Many of today's investors are unaware of Wall Street's so-called Paperwork Crisis of the 1960s, when increased trading volumes overwhelmed the industry's paper-based, back-office record-keeping. Only more sophisticated computer and administrative systems resolved the settlement crisis. Raghuram Rajan, a former chief economist at the IMF and a finance professor at the University of Chicago, says, "There's a lot of stuff that does a lot of good that we take for granted, because it's just become part of our everyday financial lives."[xxvi]

The impacts are also felt far beyond our financial lives, leading to the creation of essential products and services. Former World Bank economist and Brown University professor Ross Levine contends financial innovations are essential to the wealth of nations.[xxvii] According to Levine, railroads of the 19th century were shut out from the dominant funding sources of the day—namely banks and wealthy individuals.[xxviii] So specialized investment banks arose to better analyze the industry's massive capital needs, hastening the Industrial Revolution.

Nor could the technology, telecommunications or medical revolutions have occurred without constantly evolving financial innovations, says Dr. Levine.[xxix] Traditional commercial banks and financial markets were unclear how to evaluate the cash flows, highly technical products and unconventional management teams of these emerging industries.[xxx] Specialty venture capital firms with longer investment horizons and specialized expertise then surfaced to better evaluate and finance high-growth technology companies. In recent years, the development of a negotiated secondary market for private company securities has enabled founders and employees to sell some of their shares while allowing companies to remain private longer, thus emerging better prepared for an eventual initial public offering.

Creating innovations that positively improve people's lives won't be enough, however, to restore confidence in the tarnished financial system. The American people will only welcome innovations from a trusted source. Wall Street must first be "the repairer of the breach, the restorer of paths to dwell in."[xxxi]

Redeem

Definitions of "redeem" include "to change for the better,"[xxxii] "to restore the honor, worth, or reputation of,"[xxxiii] "atone or make amends for,"[xxxiv] and "do something that compensates for poor past behavior."[xxxv] All apply to Wall Street's challenging task ahead. In order for the financial industry to redeem itself, it will require a renewed sense of purpose, patriotism and accountability. Fortunately, this conduct is not without precedent.

America's business titans, for example, contributed to the national interest during the mobilizations of World War I and World War II, including John D. Rockefeller's support for the United War Work fundraising campaign. In a 1917 speech, Rockefeller described the united effort: "For the first time in history, people of Jewish, Catholic, and Protestant faith are standing side by side and working in closest cooperation for a great common cause."[xxxvi]

Patriotism has always seemed to be on display at the New York Stock Exchange (NYSE). Walking around the floor of the exchange, you can't help but notice how many traders' jackets are adorned with American flags. The NYSE may be a shell of its former self, now sharing the stage with numerous computerized, low-overhead competitors with names like BATS and Direct Edge—but it is still *feels* like the cradle of American capitalism and its members proudly recognize the exchange's historical significance.

In the days following the September 11 attacks, the financial industry's resolve was severely tested. As has been well documented, Wall Street responded by watching out for each other, its customers, its community and the country. When Osama Bin Laden labeled the plot an attack on capitalism, the financial community saw itself as the caretaker of something far more important than simply profits or orderly settlement of transactions. Many of the ingredients needed for Wall Street to redeem itself again were prominently on display in the days and weeks after 9/11: cooperation, honesty, service and humility.

For example, the New York Stock Exchange, a potent symbol of the American way of life, defiantly reopened the next Monday, only six days after the attacks. Even though the Dow Jones Industrial Average dropped 684 points (7.1 percent)[xxxvii] when the NYSE reopened, the important thing was that trading resumed as it had for 209 years. This feat required unprecedented coordination with numerous regulators as well as the nation's other financial exchanges. It was important that all the markets reopen on the same day to demonstrate unity and also to minimize arbitrage opportunities (i.e., exploiting of price differentials) across exchanges. While the physical exchange of the NYSE was unharmed, restoring telecommunications connectivity in lower Manhattan was a Herculean task, requiring numerous tests throughout the weekend.

Competitors also embraced each other. For example, the American Stock Exchange or AMEX, physically located a few hundred feet from the World Trade Center, was crippled in the attacks. Yet the AMEX reopened in concert with the others because of direct assistance from rival exchanges. On October 2, the American Stock Exchange issued a press release stating, "We also thank the New York Stock Exchange and Philadelphia Stock Exchange, who put aside competitive concerns to lend us trading space and support. . . . This week, as we return to our home, we've never been more proud to be citizens of this neighborhood, this city, and this nation."[xxxviii]

At an individual level, Welles Crowther, a young equities trader with Sandler, O'Neill and Partners, who died in 2 World Trade Center, exemplified service to others. Crowther, a standout lacrosse player at Boston College and an active member of the Fellowship of Christian Athletes, followed in his father's footsteps as a teenager by volunteering for his hometown Empire Hook and Ladder Company No.1 in Upper Nyack, New York.[xxxix] He has come to be known as the "man in the red bandanna," a trademark item he carried with him since childhood that was later used by eyewitnesses to confirm his heroic efforts that day.[xl]

Working on the 104th floor of the South Tower at the time of impact, Crowther is reported to have put his volunteer firefighting skills to work, saving many lives by using his calm demeanor to lead several groups of victims to safety and to extricate others. His father Jefferson Crowther acknowledged his son, "did his duty, as we say in the fire services."[xli] The body of Welles Crowther was recovered along with NYFD firefighters and emergency services personnel who had been operating a NYFD Command Center in the lobby of the South Tower and were preparing to go back up to help free other victims.[xlii]

The elder Crowther proudly explained, "People say to us, we raised him too well. I tell them, no, that boy came with the software installed. The good Lord put him here for a purpose and said at some point, "I am going to need you, Welles." Unfortunately, it was only 24 years into his life."[xliii] Despite the selfish and immoral conduct that occurred on Wall Street in the years following, it's worth remembering that Welles Crowther and others like him represented the same financial community.

In the weeks that followed, the financial industry also summoned its charitable instincts. It has been reported that Wall Street raised $6 million in less than a week after 9/11 for the families of fallen firefighters.[xliv] Four of the five largest corporate donors to 9/11 response funding were finance-related (Citigroup Foundation, Deutsche Bank Americas Foundation, General Electric Foundation, and J.P Morgan Chase/J.P. Morgan Chase Foundation.)[xlv] The NASDAQ Exchange, like many other firms and organizations, created the NASDAQ Disaster Relief Fund to provide matching contributions for victims' families, saying, "Individually, you can do a lot to help those in need. Together, we can do even more."[xlvi]

There is perhaps no greater example of Wall Street's charitable potential than the Robin Hood Foundation. Founded by legendary hedge fund manager Paul Tudor Jones, a man who once generated three-digit returns for five consecutive years,[xlvii] Robin Hood has been fighting poverty in New York City with an impact and operating efficiency few charities can match.

Robin Hood applies its management and real estate expertise by leveraging the skills, networks and brainpower of some of Wall Street's greatest minds to directly assist numerous New York City poverty relief organizations. For example, its board of directors underwrites all fundraising and administrative expenses, allowing 100 percent of all donations to reach community partner organizations.[xlviii] In addition to Mr. Jones, Robin Hood's current board of directors is stacked with hedge fund and finance heavyweights such as Steven Cohen, David Einhorn, Daniel Och, Alan D. Schwartz, David Tepper, Kenneth Langone, Glenn Durbin, Peter Borish, Julius Gaudio, John A. Griffin, Max Stone, Jes Staley and Lee S. Ainslee III.[xlix] The organization reports that it has invested over $1.1 billion since 1988 to fight poverty in New York City.[l]

Immediately after 9/11, the Robin Hood Foundation mobilized its resources and expertise to help victims' families. Since a complete list of victims' names did not exist, the foundation compiled one on its own. Using that list, the group says, "Every single family who lost someone on 9/11 received a check for $5,000 just in time for the holidays, without having to fill out an application for assistance. In some cases, the Robin Hood checks were the first funds the families received."[li] By the end of 2001, Robin Hood had distributed $15 million to 9/11 victims.[lii] Perhaps even more impressive, the foundation has remained faithful to the cause, providing $65 million over the last ten years to organizations delivering emergency assistance and support, job training and mental health services for survivors and the families of 9/11 victims.[liii]

Any reference to Wall Street philanthropy frequently invokes deep suspicions. Some question whether Wall Street gives sacrificially or for aggrandizement. Nor does philanthropy excuse any misdeeds such as those of convicted Galleon Group hedge fund founder Raj Rajaratnam, who also gave generously to the poor of his native Sri Lanka. Critics also point out that disgraced Lehman Brothers CEO Dick Fuld also once sat on the Robin Hood Foundation's board of directors,[liv] or cite founder Paul Tudor Jones' opulent homes and lavish lifestyle.[lv]

While acknowledging these concerns, it is hard to argue with Robin Hood's operational skill or deny its powerful track record of results. According to the group's website, the Attorney General of New York, for example, called the Robin Hood Relief Fund the most effective and transparent of all the 9/11 assistance funds.[lvi] It is also right to recognize Paul Tudor Jones' long-standing commitment to poverty issues and the invaluable contributions played by many Wall Street veterans whom Mr. Jones has helped to bring into the organization's orbit. It's difficult to find anything in the Judeo-Christian tradition that justifies curtailing how much good one does for others. Any such limit to beneficence would be arbitrary and misanthropic.

Robin Hood Foundation represents an example of the financial industry giving more than just its treasure but also it time and smarts— and *that* is the basis for a redeeming service culture. Our obligation to help others in every way is captured by the Hebrew concept of *tzedakah*. "There's a basic human responsibility to reach out to others. Giving of your time and your money is a statement that 'I will do whatever I can to help,'" says Rabbi Shraga Simmons.[lvii] "The Talmud asks, "Why was Adam created alone?' So that every person should say, 'The entire world was created just for me,'" he points out. This is a recognition that everything—including the needs of every other human being—was created for you. We are all caretakers of this world, responsible to deal with the problems."[lviii]

An attitude that the financial community was its "brother's keeper" or caretaker was truly prevalent in the days after 9/11. Lou Pastina, head of Floor Trading Operations at the NYSE, later explained that the exchange made the decision not to evacuate on Tuesday, 9/11, but also elected not to open either, as over 40 percent of the member firms could not get to the facility that day.[lix] Pastina praised the exchange's nurse, who "was on this trading floor administering to people that were highly stressed out that day. In my mind, she was a hero as well."[lx] In the weeks after the events, NYSE offered crisis counselors to assist workers who needed coping assistance.[lxi]

The human toll on the industry was profound, but many performed heroically. Jeff Ingber, author of *Resurrecting the Street: How US Markets Prevailed after 9/11*, explained on the tenth anniversary of the attacks, "People went through a lot of trauma. People were searching for relatives and friends who were missing. People had fears for their safety. They had young children who wanted them to come home. But they stayed. They did their job. They went about their roles with professionalism. In that way I think there were many quiet heroes, if you will, of 9/11."[lxii]

These 9/11 stories reveal one of the most important pillars of a blueprint for Wall Street's redemption: there is a tremendous reservoir of goodwill and moral conduct in the industry's rank-and-file workers. Opportunities to be "quiet" client-serving heroes abound every day, and many in the financial community have not stopped rising to that standard, albeit with little or no fanfare.

One of the things the tragedy did was to personalize the victims for people outside the financial community. The world cried at the loving remembrances provided by family members and colleagues. Those who read the tributes and profiles, such as *The New York Times* "Portraits of Grief" series, did not see Wall Street "fat cats" and moguls. Instead, they had a rare glimpse into the everyday working-class Wall Street world. This world is comprised of men and women who take the train or the ferry to work each day from middle-class suburbs and neighborhoods. They work hard to keep the gears of the free markets moving, often performing unglamorous tasks, and then dutifully return home to Little League, dance recitals and science projects. The same scene is repeated in communities all over the country by millions of average financial professionals.

The 9/11 attacks indeed caused many Americans to search for something bigger than themselves. After the financial markets had reopened earlier that day, Newsweek's Howard Fineman said that evening, "People are searching for answers beyond politics in their own souls. We have something of a Great Awakening going on in this country."[lxiii] Churches and synagogues in lower Manhattan, and around the country, were filled in the days after September 11. Shortly after the attacks, trading executive John N. Tognino teamed with New York's Fordham University to host an interfaith service attended by over 1,500 investment professionals to honor the dead, including the 204 members of the Security Traders Association of New York who were lost on that day.[lxiv]

Amazingly, neither Trinity Church, at Broadway and Wall Street, nor St. Paul's Chapel, five blocks north at Broadway and Fulton Street, were damaged in the attacks. Both are esteemed places within the financial district. The leafy Trinity Churchyard, final resting place of Alexander Hamilton, has long been a place for Wall Streeters of all beliefs seeking a respite from the workplace pressures to enjoy lunch or reflect in the fresh air. St. Paul's Chapel, part of the Episcopal Parish of Trinity Church, is Manhattan's oldest public building in continuous use, opening in 1766 and serving as a place of worship for George Washington. Mayor Rudolph Giuliani called the survival of St. Paul's one of the "miracles that help our faith to go on."[lxv]

Go on, we must. In much the same way today, Wall Street need not be imprisoned by its dark, recent past. The financial community's response to 9/11 is a reminder of what is possible when it applies its heart and mind to noble endeavors—i.e., when Wall Street brings its "best self" to work.

The symbolic ringing of the opening bell each morning at the New York Stock Exchange was an important emotional lift and sign of normalcy for both Wall Street and the nation following 9/11. The iconic ritual occupies an important place in the American psyche. It is the symbolic sound of American capitalism.

The great baseball writer Roger Angell once wrote of the game he loved, "Keep the rally alive and you have defeated time."[lxvi] Baseball is not governed by a clock. On Wall Street, however, there are always temporal limits that should serve as a reminder of both man's limitations and great promise. "In America," declared New York Senator Charles Schumer, "we start each day in our Congress and in our classrooms with the Pledge of Allegiance, and we also start it with the ringing of the bell on the floor of the stock exchange."[lxvii] Much like the seasons, the opening and closing bells on Wall Street mark an important rhythm, windowing time and renewing opportunity. Author Steve Fraser says of Wall Street, "The world is created anew each day."[lxviii] Create.

By the same token, James Cooper, the rector of Trinity Church on Wall Street, wrote in a New York Daily News op-ed to commemorate the tenth anniversary of 9/11, "I believe that in each human being lies the capacity to understand that the world is good. It is true when life would make us think otherwise, as it did on that clear September Tuesday ten years ago. Pray with me now: The world is good. Evil is the aberration. Remember to love."[lxix] Redeem.

The earth isn't heaven. We live in an imperfect world inhabited by imperfect beings. As a result, problems, even evils, build up in the financial system. Yet, when things go wrong, we are also called to repair them and restore harmony. There are solutions within the financial system's grasp—a capitalist framework worthy of preservation, recent memories of caring for others to use as a blueprint, and a moral foundation to build upon.

Notes, Chapter 2

i Peggy Noonan, "Lessons from the Recovery of 2001", *The Wall Street Journal*, April 10, 2009.

ii Henry Paulson interview, *CNBC Television*, February 15, 2012. http://www.cnbc.com/id/46252924/CNBC_EXCLUSIVE_CNBC _TRANSCRIPT_FORMER_TREASURY_SECRETARY_OF_T HE_U_S_AND_FOUNDER_OF_THE_PAULSON_INSTITUT E_HANK_PAULSON_SITS_DOWN_WITH_ANDREW_ROS S_SORKIN_TODAY_ON_CNBC_S_SQUAWK_BOX

iii Catherine Hollander, "Frank Expects to do 'Lots of Public Policy Advocacy' in Retirement", *National Journal*, December 5, 2011. http://www.nationaljournal.com/congress/quick-take-frank-expects-to-do-lots-of-public-policy-advocacy-in-retirement-20111205.

iv Ibid.

v Dr. Robert Shiller, *Yale Open Courses*, ECON-252-08: Financial Markets (2008). http://oyc.yale.edu/economics/econ-252-08.

vi Ibid.

vii Ibid.

viii Interview with William McGurn on Markets and Morality, *Religion and Ethics Newsweekly*, February 10, 2009. http://www.pbs.org/wnet/religionandethics/episodes/february-10-2009/william-mcgurn-on-markets-and-morality/2235/.

ix "Six Questions on the Cost of Corruption with World Bank Institute Global Governance Director Daniel Kaufman," *The World Bank*. http://web.worldbank.org/WBSITE/EXTERNAL/NEWS/0,,conte ntMDK:20190295~menuPK:34457~pagePK:34370~piPK:34424 ~theSitePK:4607,00.html.

x Ibid.

xi Peter and Helen Evans, "Interview with Michael Novak", *on Politics and Prayer*. http://peterandhelenevans.com/america-the-great-experiment/interviews/interview-with-michael-novak/.

xii The Holy Bible: 2 Samuel 7:8 (NIV).

xiii Dr. David Gill interview with the author, October 31, 2011.

xiv Ibid.

xv Ezra Klein, "Harvard's Liberal Arts Failure is Wall Street's Gain", *Bloomberg*, February 15, 2012.
http://www.bloomberg.com/news/2012-02-16/harvard-liberal-arts-failure-is-wall-street-gain-commentary-by-ezra-klein.html.

xvi Ibid.

xvii Adam Bryant, "The Importance of Painting a Clear Picture", *The New York Times*, November 26, 2011.
http://www.nytimes.com/2011/11/27/business/electronic-arts-chief-on-painting-a-consistent-picture.html?pagewanted=all.

xviii Rob Moll, "Doing God's Work – At the Office," *The Wall Street Journal*, February 11, 2011.
http://online.wsj.com/article/SB1000142405274870485840457613420011904460 0.html.

xix Melissa Korn, "Grads Do 'Good' for Profit", *The Wall Street Journal*, December 1, 2011.
http://online.wsj.com/article/SB1000142405297020439770457707056085982797 8.html.

xx Ibid.

xxi Dr. Robert Shiller, Yale Open Courses,
http://oyc.yale.edu/transcript/531/econ-252-08.

xxii Arjan Schutte, "Is Financial Innovation an Oxymoron?," *Forbes*, September 30, 2011.
http://www.forbes.com/sites/arjanschutte/2011/09/30/is-financial-innovation-an-oxymoron/.

xxiii Dr. Joseph E. Stiglitz remarks, *The Economist* online debate, February 23, 2010.
http://www.economist.com/debate/days/view/471.

xxiv The Financial Services Industry Cluster in New York State, *Empire State Development*, February 2006,
http://www.empire.state.ny.us/NYSDataCenter/Data/WhitePapers/ESD'sWhitePaperontheFinancialServicesIndustry.pdf.

xxv Kay Miranda, "The History of Certificates of Deposit," *eHow Money*, http://www.ehow.com/about_5031349_history-certificates-deposit.html.

xxvi James Surowiecki, "Too Clever by Half", *The New Yorker*, May 17, 2010.

http://www.newyorker.com/talk/financial/2010/05/17/100517ta_t
alk_surowiecki.

xxvii Dr. Ross Levine remarks, *The Economist* online debate, February 23, 2010. http://www.economist.com/debate/days/view/471.

xxviii Ibid.

xxix Ibid.

xxx Ibid.

xxxi The Holy Bible: Isaiah 58:12 (King James Version).

xxxii Merriam-Webster Dictionary.

xxxiii The Free Dictionary by Farlex.

xxxiv Oxford Dictionaries

xxxv Ibid.

xxxvi John D. Rockefeller 1917 speech "Fundraising", *firstworldwar.com*.
http://www.firstworldwar.com/audio/fundraising.htm.

xxxvii "How September 11th Affected the Stock Market," *Investopedia*, September 9, 2011.
http://www.investopedia.com/financial-edge/0911/How-September-11-Affected-The-US-Stock-Market.aspx#axzz1vr2Q0qeN.

xxxviii American Stock Exchange press release, October 2, 2001.

xxxix Welle's Story, Crowthertrust.org.
http://www.crowthertrust.org/welles_story.htm.

xl Greg Botelho and Maria Hinojosa, "The Man in the Red Bandanna", CNN.com.
http://www.cnn.com/SPECIALS/2002/america.remembers/stories/heroes/welles.html.

xli Jefferson Crowther interview, *USA Today* video.
http://www.usatoday.com/video/index.htm?bctid=1125481283001#/9 percent2F11 percent3A+Equities+trader+turned+firefighter+saved+many/1125481283001.

xlii Crowthertrust.org.

xliii Jefferson Crowther interview, *USA Today* video.

xliv Art Cashen Interview with 1010WINS' Juliet Papa, "New York Stock Exchange Holds Emotional Observance to Honor 9/11 Victims", *CBS New York*, September 9, 2011.

http://newyork.cbslocal.com/2011/09/09/new-york-stock-exchange-holds-emotional-observance-to-honor-911-victims/.

xlv *September 11th The Philanthropic Response,* (*The Foundation Center,* 2004), 101, http://foundationcenter.org/gainknowledge/research/pdf/911book3.pdf.

xlvi NASDAQ press release, September 21, 2001.

xlvii Meena Krishnamsetty, "Billionaire Paul Tudor Jones's Top Stock Picks", *Seeking Alpha,* December 4, 2011. http://seekingalpha.com/article/311672-billionaire-paul-tudor-jones-s-top-stock-picks.

xlviii Robinhood.org.

xlix Ibid.

l   Ibid.

li   911relief.Robinhood.org.

lii   Ibid.

liii   Ibid.

liv Maurna Desmond, "Lehman Chief: Subprime's End—Near, Pain—Not Over," *Forbes,* April 16, 2008. http://www.forbes.com/2008/04/16/rishard-fuld-lehman-markets-face-cx_md_0415autofacescan03.html.

lv Shira Ovide, "High Fees, High Life: Meet Billionaire Paul Tudor Jones," *The Wall Street Journal Blogs,* August 24, 2011. http://blogs.wsj.com/deals/2011/08/24/high-fees-high-life-meet-billionaire-paul-tudor-jones/.

lvi 911relief.Robinhood.org.

lvii "Ask the Orthodox Rabbi: Rabbi Shraga Simmons," *About.com.* http://judaism.about.com/od/orthodoxjudaismfaq/a/ask_orthodox.htm.

lviii Ibid.

lix Lou Pastina Interview, "9-11 From Inside the New York Stock Exchange", *The StreetTV,* September 9, 2011. http://www.youtube.com/watch?v=uB1AHWYv0us&feature=related.

lx Ibid.

lxi Ameet Sachdev and Evan Osnos,"Opening bell sounds amid dust, noise, tight security", *Chicago Tribune,* September 17, 2001.

http://articles.chicagotribune.com/2001-09-17/news/0109180301_1_opening-bell-wall-street-new-york-stock-exchange.

lxii Stacey Curtin, "After 9-11 Resurrecting Wall Street", *Yahoo Finance*, September 9, 2011.
http://finance.yahoo.com/blogs/daily-ticker/9-11-resurrecting-wall-street-175549615.html.

lxiii Howard Fineman interview, MSNBC *Hardball with Chris Mathews*, September 17, 2001.

lxiv Michael Scotti, "Traders Gather on 9/11 Anniversary", *Traders Magazine*, October 2011.
http://www.tradersmagazine.com/issues/24_329/traders-911-anniversary-109514-1.html.

lxv James Barron, "Trinity Church, a 9/11 Survivor, Becomes a Site of Remembrance," *The New York Times*, September 9, 2011.
http://cityroom.blogs.nytimes.com/2011/09/09/trinity-church-a-911-survivor-becomes-a-site-of-remembrance/.

lxvi Clyde F. Crews, "The Metaphysics of Baseball," *America*, April 4, 1992.
http://www.americamagazine.org/content/article.cfm?article_id=12034.

lxvii Emily Witt, "Bells, Brokers, Blue Jackets, and Bartiromo, : It's the New York Stock Exchange Show!," New York Observer, February 23, 2011.
http://www1.realclearmarkets.com/2011/02/25/bells_brokers_amp_bartiromo_it039s_the_nyse_show_110954.html.

lxviii Fraser, *Wall Street: America's Dream Palace*, 2.

lxix James H. Cooper, "Evil is real, but love still rules the day: Trinity Church's pastor offers a prayer for the city," *New York Daily News*, September 11, 2011. http://articles.nydailynews.com/2011-09-11/news/30162464_1_ground-zero-courage-love.

3 The Foundation

"Laws control the lesser man . . . Right conduct controls the greater one."
– Mark Twain

Since the onset of the financial crisis, there has been a call for more accountability. According to a November 2011 Wall Street Journal/NBC News poll, 74 percent of Americans said President Obama was not tough enough on Wall Street. In a widely discussed 2011 New York magazine piece, columnist Frank Rich also lamented, "There has been no legal, moral, or financial reckoning for the most powerful wrongdoers."[i]

Since that time, the pace of the legal reckoning has quickened. The president even pledged in his 2012 State of the Union address to "hold Wall Street accountable," announcing his intention to create a special unit of federal prosecutors and state attorneys general to accelerate financial investigations.[ii]

The moral accounting, however, remains elusive and largely unexplored. That's because values can't be universally legislated or reduced to a policy and procedures manual. Also, discussing workplace morality is still a taboo subject for some.

One thing is certain, though. The current approach is not working. The public believes the financial system has lost its moral compass. Questions surrounding how to restore moral conduct on Wall Street remain unanswered, and in many quarters, unasked.

The letter of the law is surely one important source of reform. President Obama told the news program "60 Minutes," "I can tell you, just from 40,000 feet, that some of the most damaging behavior on Wall

Street, in some cases, some of the least ethical behavior on Wall Street, wasn't illegal. That's exactly why we had to change the laws."[iii]

One example of an action that is unethical, but nevertheless legal, was when several hedge funds erected "gates" or restrictions on client withdrawals during the financial crisis. By refusing to honor client redemptions (by claiming that it was necessary to preserve the value of depressed assets for the fund's remaining shareholders), Wall Street firms placed what they wanted to do with their clients' property over what the legal owners wanted to do with it. This tactic of "blocking the exits" was (and still is) permissible. It is sanctioned in the fine print of a fund's offering documents. One consequence of denying investors access to their own money was that many of them swore off hedge fund investing altogether. Thus, the hedge fund industry's ethical breach could produce long-term costs far in excess of the short-term benefits they thought they were gaining.

It's important to recognize the limitations to a strictly positive law approach that attempts to "guardrail" Wall Street into doing what is legal. Some financial firms will undoubtedly conclude that paying repeated fines for violations is simply an acceptable cost of doing business in pursuit of fat profits. Others will prove adept at finding loopholes and go undetected. Either way, the cheaters drive up the compliance costs for the entire industry, which then passes them on to the customer.

Laws can't anticipate and proscribe every potential contingency of the incredibly dynamic financial world either. Regulations are typically focused on yesterday's problems. Regulators must also largely rely on the information provided to them. Nor can regulators possibly monitor every action and transaction or mandate sound business judgment. For example, Asian banks largely avoided the same toxic mortgage derivatives that American and European banks feasted upon not because of superior regulators but rather due to superior decision-making, choosing instead to concentrate on regional growth opportunities.[iv]

Sometimes authorities also fail to see the big picture (or refuse to acknowledge it). Despite being armed with the most comprehensive data and a small army of world-class experts, Federal Reserve Chairman Ben Bernanke was downplaying the impact of the subprime crisis as late as 2007. In a speech that year at the Federal Reserve Bank of Chicago's Annual Conference on Bank Structure and Competition, Mr. Bernanke declared, "Importantly, we see no serious broader spillover to banks or thrift institutions from the problems in the subprime market; troubled lenders, for the most part, have not been institutions with federally insured deposits."[v]

"All that said, given the fundamental factors in place that should support the demand for housing, we believe the effect of the troubles in the subprime sector on the broader housing market will likely be limited, and we do not expect significant spillovers from the subprime market to the rest of the economy or to the financial system,"[vi] Chairman Bernanke continued. "The vast majority of mortgages, including even subprime mortgages, continue to perform well. Past gains in house prices have left most homeowners with significant amounts of home equity, and growth in jobs and incomes should help keep the financial obligations of most households manageable."[vii]

Legal fixes alone will never suffice to eliminate all the ethical lapses that prevent Wall Street from achieving its full potential. Yet, more government regulation is often viewed as capitalism's only saving grace. Congressman Barney Frank told the Boston Globe, "Now, I'm a great believer in the free-market system, but I also believe that there are important values that can only be vindicated if we act together through government."[viii]

But is government really the *only* possible way we can act together to vindicate and restore the important values necessary to mend our financial wounds? Is there no nongovernmental regulatory mechanism? Indeed, there is: more self-restraint inculcated through culture-shaping institutions such as familial, civic, social, educational, market or faith communities.

Great thinkers in the past were well aware of the choice that any society must make between self-restraint and outer restraints. The eighteenth-century Irish statesman and philosopher Edmund Burke wrote, "Men are qualified for civil liberty in exact proportion to their disposition to put moral chains upon their own appetites. . . . Society cannot exist, unless a controlling power upon the will and appetite be placed somewhere; and the less of it there is within, the more there must be without."[ix] Friedrich Hayek also argued that market order depended on actors following rules of just conduct.[x]

Regulatory reform, while potentially helpful, is superficial. It primarily addresses process issues and is imposed on the industry and its workers externally. Meaningful ethical reform, however, happens internally, touches the heart, and can only originate from within Wall Street.

Enlightened Self-Interest

If nothing else, a moral self-examination by Wall Street is good for business. Alexis de Tocqueville called this "self-interest rightly understood." He recognized that government regulation alone is not enough to restrain market forces. His virtues were "more concerned with the proper functioning of the system than with the perfect order of the soul."[xi]

Tocqueville saw a distinctive attribute in the Americans he encountered on his journeys across the nation—a belief that the common welfare was necessary for one's own individual welfare. According to Tocqueville, French aristocracy, firmly entrenched with no need for utilitarian motives, would never admit to acting in their own self-interest. Instead they would claim to act nobly for the beauty or rightness of it.

Americans, by contrast, typically indulged in no such self-flattery or moral posing. As author and philosopher Michael Novak describes what Tocqueville observed, " . . . in America . . .even when people sacrificed for the city or the public good, they would always tell you they did it for their own self-interest. If you complimented their public spiritedness they would tell you, 'You don't understand; in the long run it's good for me or good for my family.'"[xii]

Long-range thinking should also inform business ethics and instill guiding principles centered on diligent self-regulation. When individuals fail to adequately regulate themselves, especially within free markets, they invite heavy-handed, one-size-fits-all outside regulation.[xiii] Given that excessive regulation, however well-intentioned, almost inevitably imposes burdensome compliance costs, reduces needed flexibility, or triggers unintended consequences, self-selected ethical compliance is far better for Wall Street's business than a heavy regulatory yoke. It is Tocqueville's "self-interest, properly understood."

Others are convinced that getting Wall Street to act in its own enlightened self-interest is as good as can be achieved. They contend that capitalism is not capable of more than self-interested restraint to keep Washington off its proverbial back.

The argument says the financial industry's pressure-filled culture is hopelessly complex and nuanced. In the 1989 movie *Black Rain*, Detective Nick Conklin, played by Michael Douglas, tells his Japanese counterpart, "Hey Matsu, New York is one big gray area."

As we now know, "gray" too often morphed into black, crossing a destructive and dangerous line during the housing securitization boom. A rotten culture ensued, featuring everything from the shirking of responsibility to blatant dishonesty.

The human mind has an enormous capacity to rationalize pervasive, unethical conduct. Moral confusion ensues. Excessive risk-taking was often seen as necessary to placate impatient shareholders, keep up with competitors, or retain key employees. Some justified it as necessary to satisfy demanding superiors or secure bonuses for the betterment of one's family. Others saw it as a short-term opportunity to sock away enough money to enable them to leave the industry and pursue other, more fulfilling, endeavors.

Harvard professor Clayton Christenson believes that many of those rationalizations start small but snowball into something much larger.[xiv] He writes, "The marginal cost of doing something 'just this once' always seems to be negligible, but the full cost will typically be *much* higher."[xv] That seemingly harmless first step often functions as the point of no return.[xvi]

The New York Times' David Brooks has written that current society often refuses to acknowledge that man is also capable of depravity.[xvii] Brooks says prior generations "grew up with a worldview that put sinfulness at the center of the human personality."[xviii] Under this traditional worldview, each recognized that he or she must "struggle daily to strengthen the good and resist the evil, policing small transgressions to prevent larger ones."[xix]

In the end, many on Wall Street were blind to the fact their conduct was inflicting severe damage on the very system that was the source of their livelihood. In short, Wall Street's debased conduct demonstrated that ethical lapses that first hurt others often boomerang and end up hurting oneself. By reversal, we can see that abiding by fixed ethical standards can save us from getting sucked into a vortex in which destructiveness and self-destructiveness become a vicious cycle.

A Universal Understanding

"If we are to go forward, we must go back and rediscover those precious values—that all reality hinges on moral foundations and that all reality has spiritual control."
– Martin Luther King Jr.

There is no dispute that enlightened self-interest wasn't enough to restrain the forces of greed on Wall Street during the housing bubble. Free markets are populated by free people, and freedom, by its nature, demands a high degree of virtue. If truth is in the eye of the beholder, it is often a slippery concept. A transcendent value system, capable of confronting any industry-specific rationalizations, is therefore needed.

Historically, western moral codes sprang from Judeo-Christian teaching. These timeless principles offer just the kind of objective, universal criteria that can be applied to today's Wall Street. The spiritual heirs of Abraham—Jews, Christians and Muslims—share certain God-mandated rules for interpersonal relationships.

Jesus taught obedience to the Mosaic code,[xx] and thus the Old and New Testaments embrace a common ethical core, the same moral law. These are the "commandments," *mitzvos* in Hebrew. Christians and Jews, for example, worked shoulder-to-shoulder in the civil rights movement, committed to ending racial injustice because they cherished the same moral truth.

That doesn't mean that everyone in the financial industry will seek guidance for their conduct from Abrahamic principles. Adherence to moral values and ethical behavior is not measured by religiosity. Identifying Judeo-Christian values as a cornerstone for ethical reform isn't an attempt to proselytize, imply self-righteous superiority, or promote one religious doctrine over another. As with anything else, there are both appropriate and inappropriate expressions of faith-centered values in the workplace. They must be translated into universal values. A secular vocabulary, respect for different beliefs, and strict compliance with Title VII's ban on workplace religious discrimination are part of an advanced regulatory framework that governs the operations of the financial industry.

Many are also justifiably skeptical of faith in this context, since the financial sector has seen its share of recent high-profile "false prophets," swindlers who wrap themselves in faith language to connect with and prey upon religious communities. Believers, on the other hand, must guard against the sin of self-righteousness—feeling that they are somehow entitled to credibility by virtue of their faith or assuming that they are always making ethical decisions simply because they are believers.

We can never forget, however, that Wall Street's current culture has been prone to abuse and fueled the worst financial collapse in seventy-five years. Deep flaws have been exposed in the prevailing decision-making model.

Both believers and non-believers can find great wisdom in Judeo-Christian ethical values that address interpersonal relations without sharing the same meta-beliefs about personal salvation. One doesn't need to believe in God to see the value of living in a society with laws that protect one against theft, fraud, etc., or one that celebrates generosity, kindness and justice. Everyone benefits from obedience to moral precepts governing how we treat each other. These virtues build a bridge for common ground.

Economic theory illustrates the potential for agreement. The Austrian economist Ludwig von Mises (1881–1973), for example, developed a comprehensive theory of human action, called "praxeology," that exploded the epistemological fallacies of the "classical school" of economic thought that pretended, for the sake of economic analysis, that humans were coldly calculating, soulless, profit-maximizing beings.[xxi] This theoretical construct (called "homo economicus") does not exist in the real world. (To give a simple example: A heartless profit-maximizer would never buy Girl Scout cookies, because he can find less expensive cookies at the local store.

Real people, however, knowingly and gladly pay an above-market price because of the non-monetary value they derive from supporting a worthy organization and their neighbor's daughter.)

Mises' "praxeology" is completely value-free, a science in which cause and effect are no more subject to human wishes than are the laws of physics or chemistry. Yet, although economic analysis per se is value-free, human life and human action are not.[xxii] Mises emphatically eschewed any attempt to separate economic action from the totality of the individual.[xxiii] According to Mises, all people have a hierarchy of values—that is, they value some options available to them more highly than others. This is a descriptive reality. The choices we make and consequent actions we take reflect our individual hierarchy of values—values informed and influenced, to a considerable degree, by our sense of right and wrong, of good and evil, as well as by what we need, want, and/or like.

Mises scrupulously avoided the prescriptive realm, never presuming to tell others what their values should be. He believed that the economist's proper role is to confine himself to the descriptive realm, to explain what policies will produce what results. If the goal is widespread prosperity, then the task of the economist is to demonstrate the means best suited to achieving that goal. In Mises' utilitarian analysis, this meant an economy based on private property.

In contrast, Moses relayed the prescriptive fundamental teaching of God's law, "Thou shalt not steal," as a divinely revealed mandate. God decreed it, so respecting others' property is right and violating it is wrong. The Bible focuses on respecting property as an act of love and mercy to one's fellow man. In other words, we honor another person's ownership of his belongings not because he has any inherent right to them, but because to take them would do him harm.

Notice that both Moses and Mises approached and addressed the issue of private property from radically different perspectives, yet arrived at the same conclusion—that humankind would reap blessings (of different types) for accepting and upholding the principle of private property.

We can all agree on the importance of having inviolate rules that govern interpersonal relations within the financial system – whether grounded in the second half of the Old Testament Decalogue, for example, or in logical utility. Whether one is spiritual, a member of an organized religion, an agnostic or an atheist, we all would prefer a Wall Street free from dishonesty or predatory behavior. Everyone who believes that greater respect for the person and property of others would improve Wall Street's conduct, and thereby help bring enhanced prosperity to the country, can appreciate the teaching value of hallowed Judeo-Christian principles.

In his category-creating book, A *Whole New Mind*, author and innovation expert Dan Pink identifies the need for holistic workplace thinking, including integration of spiritual values. Pink cites a report entitled A *Spiritual Audit of Corporate America*, published by Ira Mitroff, professor at USC's Marshall School of Business, and consultant Elizabeth Denton.[xxiv] Based upon nearly one hundred interviews, both executives and employees expressed a strong desire for faith integration, defining spirituality not as religion, but as "the basic desire to find purpose and meaning in one's life."[xxv] Mitroff and Denton also found that companies that acknowledged spiritual values and aligned them with company goals outperformed those that did not.[xxvi] "In other words, letting spirituality into the workplace didn't distract organizations from their goals," concludes Pink, "it often helped them reach those goals."[xxvii]

Judeo-Christian values are, therefore, practical tools that can effectively distinguish right from wrong and illustrate the broader impact of Wall Street's behavior on others. It is not only appropriate for Wall Street to examine itself by moral as well as legal standards, it is what the public demands. Wall Street can reassert a stewardship model that is respected by both the faithful and non-believers alike, thereby drawing the entire human family closer.

These values must be lived, though, rather than simply spoken, to earn the respect of both. There is an old cliché that says Judaism is about deed, not creed. Rabbi David Wolpe of Sinai Temple wrote during the financial crisis about the importance of incorporating Jewish ethics into business conduct: "The Rabbis of the Talmud declare: 'If one is honest in business, and earns the esteem of others, it is as if one has fulfilled the whole Torah (Mechilta, Vayassa).' Religion may begin at home, but it should never end there. If it does not move us to decency and goodness, it matters not at all what pieties we profess."[xxviii]

How can these values be lived in a secular and pluralistic financial world? In 1951, a young William F. Buckley Jr., author, television host and founder of National Review, penned his first book, entitled *God and Man at Yale*. In that ground-breaking polemic, Mr. Buckley proposed that the faculty and administration of his alma mater, Yale University, were undermining Christian values and free enterprise principles by embracing secular humanism and postmodern relativism. Buckley sought to reform higher education by identifying what he believed to be the root causes of its decay.

Buckley wrote in *God and Man at Yale*, "I do not feel that Yale should treat her students as potential candidates for divinity school. It has been said that there are those who 'want to make a damned seminary' out of Yale. There may be some who do, but I do not count myself among those. But we can, without going that far, raise the question whether Yale fortifies or shatters the average student's respect for Christianity."[xxix] Buckley believed that secular humanism did not challenge an individual or society to improve behaviors and therefore advocated for a more muscular faith in the Yale community.

We don't want to turn Wall Street into a seminary, either. The pendulum simply swung too far in the other direction on Wall Street as well during the last decade, pushing down absolute standards and thus contributing to the ethical decay. An increasingly global, consolidated and electronic Wall Street knowingly or unknowingly created an environment that marginalized the steadying hand of Judeo-Christian influences. Wall Street did not challenge itself to improve behaviors.

The financial world is quick to benchmark its participants to specific indices in order to measure performance—to let clients know how their account is doing and demonstrate the value that their manager is providing. Yet, the financial world largely avoids benchmarking its ethical and moral "performance" to any fixed or measurable standards.

Buckley lamented the fact that influential members of the Yale faculty tended to discourage religious inclinations.[xxx] Wall Street's leadership must ask itself if it discourages ethical behavior by scrubbing away important values or demonstrating ambivalence toward cultural issues.

According to a survey by the Chartered Institute of Management Accountants and the Institute of Business Ethics, 84 percent of corporate finance professionals believe that business has a moral obligation to help address global issues.[xxxi] While almost three quarters of those surveyed said that their firm had a formal code of ethics, few believed that those values were actually incorporated into strategic decision-making.[xxxii] Only 16 percent indicated that their firm reported or collected ethical benchmarking information.[xxxiii]

Wall Street could begin to repair its culture by respecting and encouraging outlets that explore ethical issues from an expanded perspective. Just as Mr. Buckley indicated that "insight into this problem cannot be had from counting the number of faculty members who believe as opposed to those that do not believe,"[xxxiv] real leadership requires embracing *all* culture-shaping institutions that encourage Wall Street to hold itself to higher standards.

A growing body of thoughtful scholarship and forums makes this examination increasingly possible. For example, David Miller, himself a former senior executive in international business and finance before embarking on theological training, heads Princeton University's Faith and Work Initiative and is the author of *God at Work*. The Yale School of Management's Christian Fellowship Club and the Yale Center for Faith and Culture conduct the Christian MBA Conference, and the Catholic Acton Institute publishes *The Journal of Markets and Morality*, a peer-reviewed academic journal.

The faith-at-work movement has operated in American business for over a century, but its recent vibrant and relevant scholarship provides a unique opportunity to integrate theory and practice into the financial ecosystem.

A Solid Foundation

Faith and finance may seem like an unlikely combination. Is there any place in America where religious and spiritual values would appear to be less at home than on Wall Street, amid plummeting public trust in the nation's markets and financial institutions? And yet, Wall Street is and always has been comprised of people of many faith traditions forming a diverse community of believers, including Christians, Jews, Muslims, Hindus and Buddhists.

According to *The New York Times*, for example, there are a "growing number of young Muslims who are disrupting Wall Street's old-boy culture."[xxxv] It is not always easy for strict practitioners of many faiths to reconcile certain financial practices with their beliefs, such as the Koran's prohibition on interest.[xxxvi] Mohamed A. El-Erian, the respected chief executive of Pimco and "one of the highest-ranking Muslims in American finance,"[xxxvii] told *The New York Times* that he would advise young Muslims to "seek the opportunities and firms that speak to their set of values, expertise and passion."[xxxviii] This process of self-discovery and inner discipline across all faiths, with Wall Street professionals asking themselves, "What do I stand for?," is an important precursor to answering the broader question, "What do *we* stand for as a firm and an industry?"

The existence of a vibrant Wall Street faith community should come as no surprise. This is not to imply that God moves people around to different industries like pieces on a chessboard. Rather, finding God in all things makes sense only if God *can* be found in all things.[xxxix]

Rev. Mark Bozzuti-Jones of Trinity Wall Street Episcopal Church wrote, "Therefore, God has occupied Wall Street long before we acknowledged it. God has been in the Zuccotti Park and has always been on Wall Street. . . . In God's occupation there is always a deeper call to truth, justice, peace and a desire for the other what we desire for ourselves."[xl]

Tim Keller, the founder of Manhattan's Redeemer Presbyterian Church, recognized this and built a church which caters to urban professionals, including many in the financial services profession. Redeemer has even created a dedicated financial services ministry through its Center for Faith and Work. Keller explains, "To some degree, it's tough to be a Christian here. But in other ways, it is the kind of soil in which Christianity does well. And that is [because] Christians are out of power."[xli]

Since faith teachings are typically not a part of Wall Street's dominant value system, the solutions can appear *more* striking and powerful. As has always been the case, faith often "grows" the best in seemingly hostile and unexpected places.

Whether they acknowledge it or not, today's bankers and traders are heirs to the likes of mutual fund trailblazer John Templeton, who elevated the role of faith in financial life. He believed that spirituality and business success were inextricably intertwined. Templeton donated freely and formed foundations to study the linkages between faith and finance.

For many years, Templeton served as the chairman of the board of the Princeton Theological Seminary and "made progress in religion the great goal of his life."[xlii] Templeton biographer Robert Herrmann wrote, "His approach goes beyond the mere 'do-goodism' of ordinary philanthropy to express a deep sense of stewardship, a commitment to use the rewards of his gift as an investor to promote the moral and spiritual progress of mankind. What better ministry could one have?"[xliii]

Early last century two important early Wall Street titans, Gustav Levy, the head of Goldman Sachs, and David J. Greene, were heavily involved in the early development of the Wall Street Synagogue, created so that Jews employed in the busy downtown area would have a place for prayer.[xliv]

Many others have followed in this tradition. They include BlackRock's respected chief equity strategist Bob Doll, who encouraged students at Yale's 2011 Christian MBA Conference to pursue excellence in family life, church life and career alike.[xlv] Doll indicated that Wall Street's pressures offered a unique forum to "live out your faith in front of colleagues."[xlvi] "How do you treat employees? Do you lose your temper?,"[xlvii] asked Doll, harkening back to the importance of deed.

The co-founders of Pittsburgh-based Federated Investors also embody these principles. The shared Roman Catholic faith of founders John F. Donahue, Richard Fisher and Tom Donnelly has influenced Federated's culture since the firm's founding in 1955.[xlviii] Mr. Donahue has been a devoted supporter of Catholic charities and education.[xlix] Over the last fifty years, numerous Federated employees have been graduates of Pittsburgh's Central Catholic High School, his alma mater.[l]

"We were absolutely convinced you could run a business and make money honestly, legitimately, with integrity, without cheating, without doing anything improper,"[li] said Donahue. "That's how we functioned. To this day, that's the way this company is run."[lii] When asked how the cofounders established a consistent ethical culture, Richard Fisher credits the teachings the cofounders learned in the Catholic Church and a desire to serve as a good role model for their children (eight in his case), always cognizant of how their actions would be seen by family members and future generations.[liii]

If there was a dean of the Wall Street faith community, though, it would surely be John C. Bogle, the venerable founder of the mutual fund organization The Vanguard Group. A Presbyterian raised in the Episcopal tradition, Bogle has been an eloquent and unwavering voice for the importance of absolute moral standards and service to others.

Bogle told a university commencement audience in 2001, "I am not at all embarrassed to mention the constructive role of religion in fostering these higher values. While I won't dwell now on the Christian values I cherish so deeply, I would note that virtually all religions preach the existence of a supreme being, the virtues of a Golden Rule, and standards of conduct that parallel the Ten Commandments. We thrive as human beings and as families, not by what faith we happen to hold, but by having faith, faith in something far greater than ourselves."[liv]

Bogle would later write in a *New York Times* editorial, "When moral relativism replaces moral absolutism, ethical standards go by the board."[lv] Dr. Kimberly Shankman, Dean of the College at Benedictine College, agrees with the need for standards: "You and I may have different conflicting ideas. You have your values, I have mine, live and let live. . . . However, there is a dark side to this apparently easy-going relativism. . . . Once we have come to see our fundamental beliefs as private and incommensurable, we lose the ability for rational engagement, and thus we likewise are more prone to be intolerant of those with whom we disagree."[lvi]

Looking back, much of Wall Street's inappropriate conduct could have been curbed if more had simply asked, what is God's standard? That's why Michael Novak insists ethical capitalism requires a "sense of sin"[lvii] to prevent men and women from going astray. Playwright and former president of the Czech Republic Vaclav Havel, a man who did not ascribe to any particular religion, explained that he too felt a "responsibility not only to the world but also 'for the world,' as though I myself were to be judged for how the world turns out."[lviii] Far too many on Wall Street failed to recognize the impact of their actions on the way the broader industry and the country would "turn out."

Leadership Failure

A virtuous culture depends heavily upon leadership. In the words of former Massachusetts Governor Michael Dukakis, "A fish rots from the head first."[lix] Or said differently, corruption at the top encourages and sanctions lawlessness at the bottom.

Where were the financial statesmen who could accept responsibility, take the industry to task, and embrace the necessary changes? Of whom could it be said, "Power never touched their soul"?

Unfortunately, Wall Street's leadership was largely absent both in terms of preventing and then later speaking out against the industry's ills—thus missing a unique opportunity to restore credibility by accepting responsibility. The dual failure of Wall Street's leadership class not only betrayed its customers, but also its rank-and-file employees who were hungry to restore the industry's good name.

Therefore, the public rightly reserved its harshest criticism for Wall Street's chiefs. A February 2010 Harris poll indicated that just 8 *percent* of respondents professed a great deal of confidence in the people running Wall Street versus even 15 percent who expressed great confidence in major corporations. Indeed the men and women of Wall Street corner offices occupied the lowest rung of public esteem in the entire business world.

Share the Same Truth

Top Wall Street executives often justified their conduct by claiming it was necessary to remain competitive with others who were "doing it that way." However, one important ingredient in developing client-centric leaders is having peers who can rein each other in and provide reminders that "we're in this thing together." A support group is needed to hold each other accountable. There is also an important fellowship aspect to asking what more one can do to serve others beyond just complying with regulations.

Alexis de Tocqueville marveled at Americans' propensity to voluntarily band together: "Americans of all ages, all stations in life, and all types of disposition are forever forming associations. There are not only commercial and industrial associations in which all take part, but others of a thousand different types—religious, moral, serious, futile . . . immensely large and very minute. Americans combine to give fêtes, found seminaries, build churches, distribute books, and send missionaries to the antipodes. Hospitals, prisons and schools take shape in that way. Finally, if they want to proclaim a truth or propagate some feeling by the encouragement of a great example, they form an association."[lx]

While some see religion as a polarizing and divisive force, it doesn't have to be this way. Vaclav Havel praised the cohesive impact of " [the] blending of classical, Christian, and Jewish elements,"[lxi] without crossing the bridge to call himself a believer. "Religion is not a zero-sum game,"[lxii] explains author and commentator Michael Medved. "A more 'Christian' Christian community is good for the Jewish community, and a more 'Jewish' Jewish community, one more in tune to its traditions and culture, is good for the Christian community,"[lxiii] says Medved. The same can be said for Wall Street—each time an individual tries to dutifully adhere to timeless moral principles and to be a financial professional "for others," it strengthens the entire financial community, regardless of any theological differences.

C.S. Lewis perhaps best explained this ethos: "Friendship is born at that moment when one person says to another 'What! You too? I thought I was the only one.'"[lxiv] He elaborated, "What draws people to be friends is that they see the same truth. They share it."[lxv]

Ethicist Dr. David Gill expresses the same sentiment through the metaphor of jazz music. Gill says that jazz musicians, unlike those in an orchestra, for example, "pass the lead around," constantly setting the table for each other.[lxvi] And in so doing, jazz musicians form a connection to each other and the audience.

Jazz musicians need to know the standards, he says—i.e., a fixed canon of songs that they can play anywhere in the world with other musicians. People of faith also share a basic set of affirmations.[lxvii] They can join in and "play" with others in any setting.[lxviii]

Every bank, hedge fund and insurance company has its own unique situation. They are also bound together, though, by a myriad of links, or "standards." This sense of mutuality and community was lost when Wall Street came to be increasingly dominated by global mega-firms and powered by impersonal technology platforms. Gone was the interconnectedness of Wall Street's close-knit partnership model based upon personal relationships and management's capital at risk, where partners and competitors helped to police each other. Finding fellow sojourners who "share the same truth" can not only restore a sense of guardianship but also reinforce the leadership resolve to pursue bold ethical reforms.

The younger generation of finance professionals recognizes the need for shared ethical values. Ethics is increasingly emphasized in leading business school curriculums. The MBA Oath, started by a group of Class of 2009 graduates of Harvard Business School, is a voluntary pledge for graduating MBAs and current MBAs to "create value responsibly and ethically."[lxix] The group's website references a coalition of over 250 schools, including students, graduates and advisors, sharing "kindred aspirations."[lxx]

A Committed Core

While camaraderie and fellowship were lost in the middle part of the last decade, Wall Street's current executives can draw strength from the fact that the industry's remnant, or committed core, cries out for principled leadership.

Throughout human history, redemption has always been possible because a remnant, a faithful portion that was temporarily overrun, steps from the darkness to check the spread of corruption. There is, and *always* has been, just such a principled portion within the financial community.

A remnant in this context refers to the core group of financial professionals who never stopped playing by the rules, behaving honorably, or putting clients and customers first. They were the good stewards of the Great Recession—and they are many, a deep reservoir. The identities of some of these individuals are known. For the most part, however, these individuals have gone unrecognized for their good work under very trying conditions.

The existence of a principled core that remained steadfastly true to its values does not neatly fit the narrative of some who prefer to cast the entire industry as black-hearted villains and modern-day robber barons. But the financial services sector includes seven million Americans working in a great variety of capacities. Tomorrow in America a loan officer, a mutual fund wholesaler, an operations manager, a compliance specialist, a financial advisor, a customer services representative, an information technology professional, an insurance agent, a research analyst, an equities trader and individuals performing hundreds of other job functions will do those jobs admirably—just as they did during the darkest days of the financial crisis.

A new Wall Street stewardship model begins with identifying those on Wall Street who behaved with honor and multiplying their influence. Learn who the heroes were. Celebrate them. Reward them. Place them in positions of power. Leaders will emerge who appeal to Wall Street's better angels. They will serve as role models and soon multiply in number. Release Wall Street to act ethically and relentlessly pursue goodness not merely out of fear of prosecution, but also out of our highest obligation to conscience. This is the way it has worked for centuries. It is the way it can work again.

Notes, Chapter 3

i Frank Rich, "Obama's Original Sin," *New York Magazine*, July 3, 2011. http://nymag.com/news/frank-rich/obama-economy/presidents-failure/.

ii Dominic Rushe, "State of the union: Obama toughens stance on Wall Street Accountability," *The Guardian*, January 24, 2012. http://www.guardian.co.uk/world/2012/jan/25/state-of-the-union-wall-street-accountability.

iii Hans Nichols, "Obama Cites Wall Street Rules, Bin Laden in Case for Re-Election," *Bloomberg*, December 11, 2011. http://www.businessweek.com/news/2011-12-13/obama-cites-wall-street-rules-bin-laden-in-case-for-re-election.html.

iv Michael Schuman, "How Asia's Bankers Avoided Crisis," *Time*, September 22, 2008. http://www.time.com/time/business/article/0,8599,1843235,00.html.

v Chairman Ben S. Bernanke speech at the Federal Reserve Bank of Chicago's 43rd Annual Conference on Bank Structure and Competition, May 17, 2007. http://www.federalreserve.gov/newsevents/speech/bernanke20070517a.htm.

vi Ibid.

vii Ibid.

viii Charles P. Pierce, "To Be Frank," *The Boston Globe*, October 2, 2005. http://www.boston.com/news/globe/magazine/articles/2005/10/02/to_be_frank/?page=full.

ix Edmund Burke, "A Letter to a Member of the National Assembly," 1791.

x Virgil Henry Storr, "Why the Market? Markets as Social and Moral Spaces, " *Journal of Markets and Morality*, Volume 12, Number 2. http://www.acton.org/sites/v4.acton.org/files/pdf/issue.pdf.

xi Ernest L. Fortin, "From Rerum Novarum to Centesimus Annus: Continuity or Discontinuity?," Faith & Reason, Winter 1991. http://www.ewtn.com/library/BUSINESS/FR91405.HTM.

xii Peter and Helen Evans, "Interview with Michael Novak," *On Politics and Prayer*. http://peterandhelenevans.com/america-the-great-experiment/interviews/interview-with-michael-novak/.

xiii Dr. David Gill interview with the author, October 31, 2011.

xiv Clayton M. Christensen, James Allworth & Karen Dillon, *How Will You Measure Your Life* (Harper Business, 2012), excerpted in

"Clayton Christensen's How Will You Measure Your Life?,"
Harvard Business School, May 9, 2012.
http://hbswk.hbs.edu/item/7007.html.

xv Ibid.

xvi Ibid.

xvii David Brooks, "When the Good Do Bad," *The New York Times*,
March 19, 2012.
http://www.nytimes.com/2012/03/20/opinion/brooks-when-the-
good-do-bad.html.

xviii Ibid.

xix Ibid.

xx The Holy Bible: Mathew 5: 17,18 (NIV).

xxi Mark W. Hendrickson, "Misesian Economics and the Bible,"
Religion & Liberty, November and December 1997.

xxii Ibid.

xxiii Ibid.

xxiv Dan Pink, *A Whole New Mind*, (New York: Penguin Group,
2005), 223.

xxv Ibid.

xxvi Ibid.

xxvii Ibid.

xxviii Brad A. Greenberg, "Madoff: Jewish, yes, but Orthodox too?,"
JewishJournal.com, December 17, 2008.
http://www.jewishjournal.com/thegodblog/item/madoff_jewish_y
es_but_orthodox_too_20081217/.

xxix William F. Buckley, Jr., *God and Man at Yale* (Chicago: Henry
Regnery Company, 1951), 3.

xxx Ibid.

xxxi "Managing responsible business: how can the finance team
contribute?," *forceforgood.com*.
http://www.forceforgood.com/Articles/Managing-responsible-
business-how-can-the-finance-team-contribute-363/1.aspx.

xxxii Ibid.

xxxiii Ibid.

xxxiv Buckley, *God and Man at Yale*, 4.

xxxv Kevin Roose, "Muslims on Wall Street, Bridging Two
Traditions," *The New York Times*, April 14, 2012.
http://www.nytimes.com/2012/04/15/business/muslims-on-wall-
street-bridging-two-traditions.html?pagewanted=all.

xxxvi Ibid.

xxxvii Ibid.

xxxviii Ibid.

xxxix John P. Milan, "The Ignatian Charism: A Spirituality for These Times." http://www.donghanh.org/main/05/tl-018_Ignatian_charism.htm.

xl Rev. Mark Bozzuti-Jones, "God the Original Occupier," *Trinity Wall Street The Fullness Blog*, October 24, 2011, http://www.trinitywallstreet.org/news/blogs/the-fullness/god-the-original-occupier.

xli Eleanor Barkhorn, "How Timothy Keller Spreads the Gospel in New York City, and Beyond," *The Atlantic*, February 21, 2011. http://www.theatlantic.com/entertainment/archive/2011/02/how-timothy-keller-spreads-the-gospel-in-new-york-city-and-beyond/71301/.

xlii Robert L. Herrman, *Sir John Templeton: Supporting Scientific Research for Spiritual Discoveries*, (Philadelphia: Templeton Foundation Press), 5. http://www.sirjohntempleton.org/pdf/SirJohnBio_full.pdf.

xliii Ibid.

xliv Marvin Greisman, "The Orthodox spirit of Wall Street since 1929," *Downtown Express*, July 22-28, 2005. http://www.downtownexpress.com/de_115/theorthodoxspiritof.html.

xlv Rob Moll, "Doing God's Work – At the Office", *The Wall Street Journal*, Feb 11, 2011. http://online.wsj.com/article/SB10001424052748704858404576134200119044600.html.

xlvi Ibid.

xlvii Ibid.

xlviii Jeffrey L. Rodengen, *New Horizons: The Story of Federated Investors*, (Fort Lauderdale: Write Stuff Enterprises, 2006), 144.

xlix Ibid., 144.

l Ibid., 45

li Patricia Sabatini, "Federated Buys Kaufmann Fund," *Pittsburgh Post Gazette*, October 21, 2000. http://old.post-gazette.com/businessnews/20001021federated5.asp.

lii Ibid.

liii Richard Fisher interview with the author, April 25, 2012.

liv Commencement Address by John Bogle, Susquehanna University, May 13, 2001. http://www.vanguard.com/bogle_site/sp20010513.html.

lv John C. Bogle, "There Were Once Things One Just Didn't Do," *The New York Times*, March 16, 2012. http://www.nytimes.com/roomfordebate/2012/03/15/does-morality-have-a-place-on-wall-street/there-were-once-things-one-just-didnt-do.

lvi Dr. Kimberly Shankman, "Reason, Truth and Democracy: The Enlightenment and Its Alternatives," *The Gregorian*, November/December 2011.

lvii Peggy Noonan, "Capitalism Betrayed," *The Wall Street Journal*, June 28, 2002. http://online.wsj.com/article/SB122418798051441971.html.

lviii Edward E. Ericson, "Living Responsibly: Vaclav Havel's View," *Religion and Liberty*, Volume 8, Number 5. http://www.acton.org/pub/religion-liberty/volume-8-number-5/living-responsibly-v percentC3 percentA1clav-havels-view.

lix "On Language; Rot at the Top," *The New York Times Magazine*, September 11, 1988. http://www.nytimes.com/1988/09/11/magazine/on-language-rot-at-the-top.html?pagewanted=all&src=pm.

lx Virginia A. Hodgkinson ed. and Michael W. Foley ed., The Civil Society Reader (Tufts University Press, 2003) 123.

lxi Ibid.

lxii Michael Medved speech at the Grove City College Vision and Values Conference, April 19, 2012. http://www.visionandvalues.org/2012/04/when-im-64-israel-american-conservatives-since-1948/.

lxiii Ibid.

lxiv http://www.goodreads.com/author/quotes/1069006.C_S_Lewis.

lxv Ibid.

lxvi Gill interview with the author, October 31, 2011.

lxvii Ibid.

lxviii Ibid.

lxix www.mbaoath.org.

lxx Ibid.

4 Sprinklers

We maintain that there are many admirable people in the financial industry, individuals whose professional conduct is beyond reproach. These are the unsung heroes of Wall Street. Unfortunately, their goodness is often eclipsed by the "bad apples"—those who have strayed into reckless, unethical or criminal conduct. One might wish that the good would dominate the bad on Wall Street, that internal and external controls would provide effective barriers against misconduct, but that hasn't happened. Human beings are not puppets on the strings of wise and good controllers. Like it or not, we all have the ability to make bad decisions—that is, to err, to screw up (to sin, if you will).

The questions then become: What conditions have emerged in recent years that made it easier for Wall Streeters to stray from the "straight and narrow"? Ultimately, of course, the heart of the problem is the wrong choices made by individuals, but what institutional and technological factors might have facilitated Wall Street misconduct?

Katherine Leary Alsdorf, the founder and executive director of the Center for Faith and Work (a ministry of Manhattan's Redeemer Presbyterian Church), hypothesizes that Wall Street's emphasis on specialization contributed to the problem.[i] Wall Street's high-pressure, skills-based job functions have become so specialized that it fosters a "heads down" attitude. Employees are increasingly "math wizards," operating in a mental realm devoid of social or moral context. Similarly, managers rise up through narrow functional silos where their performance is evaluated on strictly quantitative criteria.

Many on Wall Street thought that as long as they were personally living up to high moral and ethical standards in their work, it was enough.[ii] The financial industry as a whole, including both those who abused the system and those who behaved with honor, failed to recognize how profoundly Wall Street's actions affected the broader world, concludes Ms. Leary Alsdorf.[iii] Both largely missed the big picture.

An essential ingredient in a Wall Street reform agenda is, therefore, a bedrock belief that each financial professional has a stake in the future of Wall Street beyond their own department, business unit, trading desk or firm. Each needs to see himself not just as an independent agent or part of a particular firm's team, but as an important member of Wall Street's broader society with a personal stake in the Street's reputation. This requires constantly evaluating one's own conduct in light of how it colors people's perceptions of the industry as a whole, and recognizing that the impact of one's business decisions may be far-reaching.

In the past, direct interactions with clients gave Wall Streeters useful, real-time feedback on how they were being perceived. However, in recent years, Wall Street workers have become increasingly detached from their clients. The proliferation of technology was an important contributing factor in disconnecting people from each other.

This is undoubtedly true of society as a whole. Researchers from the University of Maryland found, " . . . after a short period of cellphone use the subjects were less inclined to volunteer for a community service activity when asked, compared to the control-group counterparts. The cell phone users were also less persistent in solving word problems— even though they knew their answers would translate to a monetary donation to charity."[iv] The atomistic psychology of cell phone usage reduced users' "desire to connect with others or to engage in empathic and prosocial behavior."[v]

On Wall Street, however, technology, financial engineering and globalization diluted the sense of accountability, with profound financial and economic consequences. Traders felt more emboldened to take excessive risks because they didn't have to face the disapproval of clients and shareholders who shouldered the losses. Throughout the financial world, email, computerized trading platforms and programs, structured investment vehicles, and other innovations served to impersonalize the financial business, and weakened the tie between a financial professional's actions and the personal impact those actions had.

Financial innovation, for example, should also be accompanied by education. Personal financial advisors have an essential educational role to play in a world of increasingly complex investment and insurance products. The most effective financial advisors meet regularly with their clients, product providers and investment managers as part of the education process.

Broken interpersonal relationships, however, have become part of a disturbing trend on Wall Street that reached a tipping point during the financial crisis. Vanguard founder Jack Bogle observed, " . . . professional relationships with clients have been recast as business relationships with customers. I do not regard that as progress."[vi]

The origins of this attitude can be traced back to May 1, 1975, the day on which US Securities and Exchange Commission (SEC) mandated the deregulation of the brokerage industry. That event, which came to be known as "May Day," transformed the industry by paving the way for the reduction of commissions on stock trades. The new policy replaced Wall Street's old collusive, cartelistic, fixed-price schedule with wide-open competition. While spawning the discount brokerage revolution and empowering individual investors, the decision yielded other consequences. Most notably, big Wall Street firms shifted their focus to institutional customers, thereby weakening longstanding ties with individual customers. Today, many large brokerage firms discourage their financial advisors from adding new clients below $250,000[vii] in assets in order to concentrate on higher-margin, well-heeled customers.

During the housing boom, many on Wall Street said, "It's not my job to protect people from themselves," referring to homeowners, housing speculators and institutional purchasers of securitized products. Yet, the financial industry was not simply watching from afar. It was a willing, active accomplice in the events—setting the boom in motion and later doing nothing to slow it down when things clearly started to go sideways. It's worth remembering that bartenders can be charged with criminal recklessness for knowingly or intentionally serving an inebriated patron.

In theory, large institutions should have been better able to assess the risks of complicated products and strategies. Some of the mortgage derivatives created during the securitization boom were so complex, however, that few people actually understood them. Some professional investors just assumed that someone else must understand the products. Everyone else was buying them, and the credit ratings agencies blessed them, so there was no need to worry. It was a suspension of common sense and a misplaced confidence that advanced alchemy could somehow reduce risk and eliminate the need to think for oneself.

In other cases, sophisticated professional investors diligently analyzed publicly available data and simply reached the conclusion that mortgage securities would continue to increase in value. In fairness, default rates on investment-grade mortgage securities were historically very low. Experienced investors with this optimistic view of the housing market enthusiastically engaged in arms-length derivatives transactions with counterparties who held the opposing view—producing winners and losers. So be it. We are not suggesting that morality can be injected into trading systems. However, when the taxpayer is ultimately one of the losers, on the hook for potentially unlimited losses, it changes the dynamic completely.

Derivatives and securitization, in and of themselves, are not inappropriate. Assuming the disclosures are accurate and marketing practices are transparent, there is nothing wrong with market makers connecting clients who want different exposures. Credit default swaps (CDS) can perform a valuable function by hedging non-marketable financial exposure to troubled corporations or nations. Customized over-the-counter swaps often better meet the needs of hedgers than standardized futures contracts. If, for example, you are a large creditor or counterparty of a company that is teetering on the edge of bankruptcy, buying credit default swap protection can be prudent risk management. Many industries such as electric power providers also routinely use derivatives to manage commercial risks for the benefit of customers.

As was discussed in the Chapter 2, true financial innovation can promote tremendous progress. Poorly designed engineering or clever products devised for improper motives, however, produce great instability. Indeed, mortgage derivatives almost burned down Wall Street's entire house during the financial crisis of 2008. Many of the financial instruments conceived during the housing boom were designed for one reason: to generate leveraged profits rather than to produce any real economic benefit.

Nobel Prize-winning economist Joseph Stiglitz takes these destructive financial instruments to task for their limited economic utility: "There is also ample evidence that they have been useful in accounting, regulatory and tax arbitrage, activities that may enhance the profits of the companies employing them, but not necessarily the efficiency of the economy. They have helped governments and firms hide their financial doings from taxpayers and investors. And those benefiting from such deception have been willing to pay amply for it, with large profits to the innovators, even if society as a whole loses."[viii]

Ridiculously, some contended that these innovations made the financial system stronger by enhancing the ability to identify and control risks. Among those making such arguments was former Federal Reserve Chairman Alan Greenspan, who contended in 2005, "The use of a growing array of derivatives and the related application of more-sophisticated approaches to measuring and managing risk are key factors underpinning the greater resilience of our largest financial institutions. . . . Derivatives have permitted the unbundling of financial risks."[ix] Unfortunately, although perhaps understandably, almost everyone in the financial industry accepted these statements at face value, because they assumed that the powerful chairman of the Federal Reserve System was in a better position than anyone to evaluate the risks. In truth, risk was not eliminated because it was securitized.

Beginning in 1998, US commercial banks could determine their regulatory capital requirements for financial market risk exposure using value-at-risk (VaR) models.[x] These complex models proved woefully inadequate, though, at predicting future risks. Actual trading losses in 2008 quickly overwhelmed flawed model projections based on probability assumptions.

That's because the housing boom produced a plethora of poorly designed financial instruments. At the top of the list was a host of dubious mortgage products, such as negative amortization and interest-only loans, that were designed to maximize buyers' short-term purchasing power with no regard for the disastrous long-term consequences. Mortgage lenders, particularly nonbank lenders, then developed sophisticated approval software designed specifically to rush buyers through a faux underwriting approval process.

The crowning folly was the bundling of those shaky mortgages into tradable securities. Securitization facilitated the marketing and packaging of subprime loans, while structured investment vehicles were created to keep those problematical securities off of bank balance sheets. This is one of the dirty secrets of the financial crisis: flawed financial engineering infected financial statements in the form of poor and sometimes even improper accounting.

Global organizations themselves became more complex, raising questions whether any executive can adequately oversee such complicated enterprises. Some would say that the organizational design suggests a move toward concealment. At the very least, it promotes a lack of accountability. Take the example of MF Global, the bankrupt derivatives and commodities broker at the heart of a current investigation surrounding its possible improper use of segregated client funds. Multiple regulators had various forms of jurisdiction over MF Global. Commissioner Jill E. Sommers, a member of the US Commodity Futures Trading Commission (CFTC), told a Congressional hearing, "We can't overemphasize the complexity of MF Global's books and regulators."[xi]

As this is written, prosecutors have yet to uncover a smoking gun that would result in criminal prosecutions for MF Global executives. The company apparently fell victim to the "fog of war" as things chaotically unraveled in the firm's final days, including the transfer of cash from customers' segregated accounts. Even if what happened turns out not to have been illegal, the firm's complexity easily outstripped its inadequate risk controls. The books were simply too complicated.

Financial engineering run amok, in all its forms, reveals one of Wall Street's most dangerous and prevalent character flaws: hubris. It is an area where Judeo-Christian values have great prescriptive relevance for the financial industry and can help to steer Wall Street back toward less risky and reckless practices.

The financial crisis glaringly illustrated the need for humility and acceptance of human limitations—not an easy sell on Wall Street. Author Tom Wolfe scornfully dubbed its participants "Masters of the Universe" for good reason in his influential novel *The Bonfire of the Vanities*. Confidence is certainly needed to trade effectively in such a competitive and pressure-filled environment. But as it says in the Bible, "Great men are not always wise."[xii] The two should not be confused.

After the 1987 stock market crash, so-called "circuit breakers" were instituted to slow down market activity during major declines and surges, creating a "timeout" from trading to allow cooler heads to prevail. In the same way, timeless values can help Wall Street to regularly slow down its overconfident impulses.

Without that check, unbounded creativity can become harmful. Man has boundaries, and there is such a thing as information overload. Trading glitches such as the 2010 "Flash Crash" (when stocks plunged roughly 1000 points in a few minutes) and the order execution snafus in the Facebook IPO damage investor psychology and call into question whether current technology can even support Wall Street's current level of complexity. As in other industries, engineering and technological ingenuity can be destructively misdirected, and human intelligence is prone to self-selection biases.

Dr. Woody Brock, economist and author of *American Gridlock*, identifies the delusion that often accompanies the arrogance of modern-day alchemy: "Excel spreadsheets plus the wealth of information accessible from the Internet is proving very dangerous to informed debate. 'Factoids' are confused with serious logic, and young people are all but clueless about Hume's imperative: You cannot data-crunch your way to the Truth. Ever."[xiii]

The dominant belief on Wall Street is that added complexity enhances competitive advantage. The assumption is that while additional layers of complexity may cause others to stumble, superior intellect and resources will always enable one's own firm to ultimately prevail. Within this worldview, culture and values are thus rarely seen as important sources of competitive advantage. "Smartness" often crowds out other important human virtues like empathy and compassion.

We need a financial system in which both participants and regulators better understand the risks. We also need a financial system that acknowledges human limitations in measuring and predicting future risks. In his acclaimed book *Against the Gods*, author Peter L. Bernstein traces finance's long history of advancements in risk forecasting. Yet, the financial crisis of 2008 demonstrates that effective forecasting remains beyond the financial wizards' grasp. It is still possible for modern Icaruses to fly too close to the sun.

As financial products and organizations became more complex and esoteric, they easily overran an outdated financial oversight system. Both non-banking lending and derivatives markets developed faster than regulators could police or even evaluate. "A regulatory regime basically crafted in the wake of a twentieth-century economic crisis—the Great Depression—was overwhelmed by the speed, scope, and sophistication of a twenty-first–century global economy," declared President Obama.[xiv]

In some ways, financial engineering is like blood doping in professional cycling, whereby the innovators are inherently one step ahead of techniques for detection. It is essential, then, that innovations, just like the financial professionals who design them, begin to function as part of a larger ethical ecosystem. We need what the Bible calls "honest measures."[xv]

Wall Street, therefore, can't be allowed to hide behind complexity or avoid providing a clear roadmap for how to "disarm" any innovations that could "go rogue" under extreme conditions. As part of the product-approval process, financial innovators should provide regulators with analysis tools for rigorous ongoing monitoring. The SEC has developed its own sophisticated internal computer system to analyze and flag monthly returns from thousands of hedge funds,[xvi] for example, but regulators can't be expected to underwrite all the necessary development costs in an ever-escalating "space race."

Financial innovation is like the space program in another respect: Shooting a rocket into space is only half the mission. It must also be equipped to safely return to earth! This includes processes that allow regulators to understand the dependencies between financial institutions and that enable orderly liquidation.

Many areas of the financial system have been slowly parachuting back to earth. The long healing process has begun. Since 2009, US banks have steadily improved their capital position—increasing loan loss reserves, reducing leverage ratios, and paring back exposure to troubled European periphery nations such as Portugal, Ireland, Spain, Greece and Hungary. Today, US banks hold more of their Tier 1 capital in the form of high-quality common equity and have also limited their dependence on short-term wholesale funding. Most financial institutions will also be required to raise additional capital to comply with stricter, phased-in international banking standards known as Basel III. Elsewhere in corporate America, balance sheets are flush with cash, and companies have generally sworn off overpaying for acquisitions (at least for now) in massively leveraged transactions.

In addition, conditions have improved on the lending side as well. While lax bank regulation was previously permitted, if not encouraged, the so-called "shadow" or unregulated nonbank lending segment, has essentially disappeared. Bank regulators also began cracking down hard on the remaining traditional lending institutions, and Congress passed the sweeping Dodd-Frank Wall Street Reform and Consumer Protection Act (Dodd-Frank) in 2010 giving the Federal Reserve and the Federal Deposit Insurance Corporation (FDIC) greater authority to adequately regulate nonbank lenders. US financial institutions have been recapitalized, in part, because of prudential regulation. The system is stronger and safer because of these reforms.

The ballooning financial regulatory apparatus contains its own flaws and dangers, though. Some argue that capital and liquidity requirements have become too restrictive, forcing already heavily regulated Main Street banks to pay for the prior bad acts of their larger Wall Street competitors. When the regulatory regime dramatically expands, unintended consequences inevitably follow. James Madison warned against the "multiplicity and mutability of laws," while Winston Churchill declared, "If you have ten thousand regulations you destroy all respect for the law."

More regulation and overlapping regulatory authorities are indeed a tax on Wall Street's—and the economy's—potential. It's unclear, for example, why the Federal Reserve Bank of New York continues to have bank oversight responsibilities. Wouldn't it make more sense for the Fed to focus on monetary policy and allow other agencies to handle bank supervision? At the same time, politicians could come to see banks as the current incarnation of "Big Tobacco," a deep-pocketed revenue source.

"They're creating $300 million worth of jobs in the new consumer financial protection bureau which I don't think is going to do much for productivity in America,"[xvii] Staples founder Tom Stemberg told Fox News. "We're creating all kinds of jobs trying to live up to Dodd-Frank . . . and those jobs don't create much productivity."[xviii]

The regulatory system can't be used as a tool to punish critics or dissenters either. Jamie Dimon, the CEO of the nation's largest bank, J.P. Morgan Chase, said in a lengthy 2012 letter to shareholders, "Many bankers would have loved to support proper reform. But it is hard to support something when you were not involved in the process in a meaningful way. In fact, at a bankers' meeting with one hundred bank CEOs in the room, 70 percent–80 percent said they were afraid to speak up because of potential retribution from the regulators and examiners."[xix]

The times demand regulatory consistency. The Latin root of "regulation"—*regula*—means "rule" and also connotes regularity—that is, predictability and constancy as opposed to arbitrariness and privilege. For example, during the fall of 2008, hedge funds were forced to grapple with hastily drafted regulations that imposed a three-week ban on the short-selling of selected financial institutions.

The short-sale ban was akin to moving the goalpost in the middle of the game for certain types of funds, and it set off a disruptive chain reaction of unintended consequences, such as wreaking havoc in the convertible bond market. The policy itself did not prevent financial stocks from plunging lower because it failed to address the underlying problem—toxic assets polluting bank balance sheets. Many institutions were forced to sell securities they could no longer hedge. The ban demonstrated the difference between thoughtful, effective regulation and politicized, ad hoc rule-making.

The policy's principle architect, former SEC Chairman Christopher Cox, later confessed that the commission had reluctantly imposed the ban under intense pressure from Treasury Secretary Henry Paulson and Federal Reserve Chairman Ben Bernanke.[xx] Mr. Cox conceded, "While the actual effects of this temporary action will not be fully understood for many more months, if not years, knowing what we know now, I believe on balance the Commission would not do it again. The costs appear to outweigh the benefits."[xxi]

No market can function without clear rules of the game, and no true defender of free markets is dogmatically "anti-regulation." The reality is, though, that the public's trust in Wall Street has been shattered. Fewer than 35 percent of Americans believe that "the stock market is a fair and open way to invest one's money."[xxii] An image makeover alone won't be enough to overcome that degree of skepticism.

Instead, Wall Street needs, and in some ways depends upon, a credible regulatory framework—now more than ever. Fraud and unconstrained credit are the two essential ingredients of financial bubbles. On both counts, risks remain elevated. Yet, the last thing Wall Street can afford is another bubble. The consequences would be devastating, producing a generation of disgusted investors much like those forever scarred by the Crash of 1929. Another crisis would also guarantee even greater government intrusion into the financial sector.

A regulatory "race to the bottom" is simply not in the best interests of financial markets. That race, says respected law professor William Black, can only be won by those who stop running.[xxiii] "There is no greater killer of jobs than elite financial fraud," concludes Professor Black.[xxiv]

He correctly points out that equities listed in the US have historically traded at a premium to other exchanges.[xxv] Investors have been willing to pay more because of their perception of the rule of law and the watchful eye of US regulators. US issuers, in turn, historically have been able to raise more capital at favorable terms.

But we should never take this goodwill premium for granted or assume that it can't be swiftly eroded by "crony capitalism." Already various shady practices have weakened it. For example, there is no excuse for the "robo-signing" scandal, where banks rushed to foreclose on houses without properly reviewing, processing, recording and transferring legal titles to properties. Banks can't argue for the sanctity of contract while themselves cutting contractual corners through inadequate review. The issue of clear legal titles to property is indispensable to a thriving capitalist economy, as the Peruvian economist Hernando de Soto explained in his best-seller *The Mystery of Capital*. We either restore the clarity and inviolability of titles to property, or our capitalist system breaks down.

The foreclosure process is supposed to be measured and accurate, because expelling people from their homes is traumatic and hurtful. Sloppy "robo-signing" procedures were at best insensitive and unnecessary—and at worst cruel and illegal.

The recent case of MF Global is a vivid example of why so many people distrust Wall Street. In MF Global's final days before seeking bankruptcy protection, $1.2 billion in customer funds "disappeared." These were the firm's "loyal" remaining customers who did not pull their accounts when rumors first started to swirl about the company's capital position and its teetering, large, proprietary bet on European sovereign debt. While the bankruptcy trustee ultimately recovered a portion of customer funds, some 38,000 customers were forced to labor over confusing seventeen-page claim forms just to get in line to recoup their own money.[xxvi]

While Wall Street thinks that many of the new regulations are too burdensome, many people outside the financial community say that they don't go far enough. Some are frustrated by what they see as an overly cautious approach to high profile prosecutions of major investment banks. Others say that the US Securities and Exchange Commission's dependence on congressional appropriations (rather than fees and fines it collects itself) ensures that the agency is perpetually underfunded and restricts it ability to operate as an independent federal agency.[xxvii] There are also those who claim that by publicly admitting its funding challenges, the SEC emboldens financial wrongdoers.[xxviii]

In the eyes of its critics, regulators were "asleep at the switch," failing to uncover misdeeds like the epic Bernie Madoff fraud. *Time Magazine* named former SEC Chairman Christopher Cox as "One of 25 People to Blame for the Financial Crisis," citing lax enforcement.[xxix] However, just as casting the entire financial industry as modern-day "robber barons" is unsophisticated and lazy analysis, so too are attempts to broadly portray regulators as unengaged.

In late 2011, the SEC responded to the criticism in a press release: "During the last 2½ years, the agency has filed 36 separate actions in its financial crisis-related cases against 81 defendants—nearly half of whom were CEOs, CFOs and senior corporate executives, resulting in approximately $1.97 billion in disgorgement, penalties, and other monetary relief obtained."[xxx] Some say that the fines associated with many of these settlements are not punitive enough. However, the SEC has been hamstrung by the existing statutory framework.[xxxi] As a result, SEC Chairwoman Mary S. Shapiro has asked Congress for the authority to impose stiffer monetary penalties.[xxxii]

The SEC is tasked with performing one of the most challenging tasks in the entire regulatory world. It must determine how to implement both the massive Dodd-Frank law and the abuse-prone Jumpstart Our Business Startups (JOBS) Act, including drafting rules, soliciting public comment, and fielding requests for exceptions. In addition to its existing duties, the SEC is also evaluating new rules for money market funds, credit-rating agencies, credit default swaps, and high-frequency trading, to name just a few.

Financial markets need a credible referee. It's often said that the best referee in a boxing match is one you don't notice—not because he isn't doing his job, but rather because the referee's gravitas causes both fighters to obey all commands without having to be constantly separated. While the financial oversight function is often unglamorous work, it is absolutely essential and deserves respect.

"Perp Walks"

Many critics are unsatisfied, though, since there have not been enough financial "perp walks"—that is, high-profile arrests and prosecutions of those responsible for the financial meltdown. In contrast, a wave of successful criminal prosecutions followed the collapse of the savings and loan industry in the late 1980s, resulting in nearly eight hundred bank officials going to jail.[xxxiii] Several of those cases, such as that of Lincoln Savings and Loan chief Charles Keating, included racketeering charges that carried lengthy prison sentences.

However, no CEO of a major Wall Street firm has thus far been criminally prosecuted. Accountability, therefore, seems unevenly distributed.

Over the last thirty years, federal law has criminalized more and more conduct.[xxxiv] Over four thousand offenses now carry criminal penalties under the United States Codes, a one-third increase since 1980.[xxxv] The availability of more crimes gives prosecutors more discretion and more leverage against defendants.[xxxvi] The option of throwing the proverbial "kitchen sink" of charges at a defendant is a very powerful tool in plea negotiations, yet the number of federal financial fraud prosecutions has been falling steadily for twenty years.[xxxvii]

A major stumbling block to financial criminal prosecutions is the difficulty of proving that the defendant had the intent to defraud or *mens rea* (Latin for a "guilty mind"). While the standards for intent have gotten murkier with the explosion in number of federal crimes, an intent bar must be cleared nonetheless. Critics say such a standard has allowed CEOs to plead ignorance and hide behind the "I didn't know" defense. At one firm after another, top executives have claimed to lack knowledge of their firm's daily operations, casting themselves as detached visionaries.

Regulators can require more executive sign-offs and certifications on things like large transfers of customer funds or large exposure trades. This would create a greater paper trail so that we have a better sense of who knew what and when, functioning like an aircraft's "black box," or flight data recorder. But we can't criminalize flawed analysis, such as the view that housing prices would continue to rise as far as the eye can see, with perfect hindsight. In addition, some of the conduct now prohibited under Dodd-Frank and other regulations was simply not illegal at the time.

As maddening as it may be that there have been no prosecutions of major bank executives, there is simply no way to dispense with a requirement of intentional criminal conduct. The alternative would criminalize willful misconduct, *as well as* poor business judgment or honest mistakes. Furthermore, many investors would automatically equate negative market outcomes, such as "my 401(k) is down 20 percent," with unethical or illegal conduct.

The Bible was an important inspiration for many modern judicial codes. In the words of President Barack Obama, "Our law is by definition a codification of morality, much of it grounded in the Judeo-Christian tradition."[xxxviii] While many want "scalps" or retribution, including politicians in an election year, the honorable and patient administration of justice is a critically important value. Financial prosecutions take time, as they require specialized expertise, investigative skill, and considerable support staff.

That doesn't mean that wrongdoers should go unpunished, though. Top financial executives should not get a free pass just because intent to defraud can't be easily established. It just means that prosecutors must look in specific, sometimes politically unpopular, places.

The Workarounds

Given the intent requirements, regulators strategically pursued other avenues. Honing in on insider trading prosecutions as its deterrence tool of choice, the SEC secured over fifty criminal convictions in 2010–11.[xxxix] The SEC's Market Abuse Group orchestrates insider trading investigations, closely monitoring suspicious activity, typically ahead of takeover and earnings announcements. The insider trading crackdown and the tools utilized to secure convictions produced a chilling effect that reverberated throughout the financial community.

Unlike many financial fraud cases that hinge on parsing highly technical information, insider trading cases are less complicated to prove and easier for juries to understand. Prosecutors must demonstrate that the information is "material," meaning something a reasonable investor would find important. They must also show that the person knew that it was confidential, non-public information, thereby breaching a fiduciary duty to the source.

There is a misconception among some that the SEC is a criminal justice agency. The commission brings civil actions in federal court or before an administrative law judge, the penalties for which include fines, the disgorgement of illegal profits, or banishment from the industry. The commission coordinates closely with law enforcement officials, since both criminal and civil actions are regularly brought in the same case. US Attorneys from the Department of Justice, aided by FBI investigators, however, are tasked with conducting federal criminal prosecutions. Preet Bharara, the United States Attorney in Manhattan, has spearheaded many of the insider trading prosecutions.

For the first time, prosecutors and FBI investigators began deploying clandestine wiretaps in insider trading cases, a tactic typically reserved for terrorist and organized crime investigations. Agents dubbed one high-profile operation "Perfect Hedge," since insider traders could never lose by virtue of their information advantage.[xl] These successful prosecutions pieced together information to establish a network of insider tips that included financial, technology and pharmaceutical company employees, directors, consultants, analysts and money managers—and resulted in sixty convictions[xli] and guilty pleas. Separate juries convicted all seven defendants who rolled the dice and went to trial in connection with the "Perfect Hedge" insider trading investigation.[xlii]

Some say that the stepped-up campaign to root out insider trading has made it more difficult for traders to know where the legal line now lies in this area. Many firms place thousands of trades each day, sometimes buying and selling the same security multiple times, and aggregate information from hundreds of research sources to arrive at investment decisions. Others contend that the SEC has overreached in recent years by weakening the fiduciary duty requirements, thereby potentially ensnaring a larger pool of defendants.[xliii]

Securities markets depend on the vibrant flow of information, and those that do their homework should be rewarded. There is a difference, however, between diligent, lawful research and a privileged circle of insiders—and the distinction is not as blurry as some suggest. While it is inevitable that investment professionals will stumble upon non-public information, they have a clear duty to refrain from trading in those instances. The reality is that some traders try to cultivate personal relationships for the abusive purpose of unfair access.

Yes, evolving standards of insider trading jurisprudence can present a challenge for investment professionals, and cooperating witnesses trying to save their own hide can muddy the fairness of these cases. Insider trading also can't be as vaguely defined as it is the United Kingdom, for example. Common sense should be applied to federal sentencing guidelines, and regulators must be very prudent in commencing investigations that can result in investor redemptions, exorbitant legal costs, and rising insurance premiums—even though no charges are ever subsequently filed. That being said, the SEC and other regulators have found an effective conduit in insider trading to send the entire financial industry a strong enforcement message.

In a world where Wall Street has invested hundreds of millions of dollars to facilitate real-time decision-making, it frequently adopts the exact opposite approach to compliance-related matters. It's time to also adopt a real-time compliance mindset and invest in internal risk-management controls.

Steven A. Cohen, founder of the $14 billion hedge fund SAC Capital Advisors LLC, acknowledged the confusion that sometimes surrounds insider trading: "The answer is when you're trading securities, it's a judgment call. Whatever the compliance manual says, it probably doesn't take into account every potential situation."[xliv] Cohen indicated he often seeks counsel from the fund's lawyer to determine whether something constitutes inside information.[xlv] That is a sensible approach. When in doubt, ask!

While traders are still ultimately on the hook for their actions, getting the expert advice of compliance officers or firm counsel *before* placing a trade can go a long way to stopping improper practices. If the information is so time-sensitive that one can't wait for a compliance opinion or clearance, it's probably not information that should be used.

As a practical matter, insider trading enforcement is virtually non-existent in many of the world's markets. In others, it is not even expressly prohibited. Yet, regulatory oversight designed to level the playing field is one of the fundamental reasons US securities markets have enjoyed a unique premium relative to others.

"Stock trading takes place on anonymous exchanges, so the trader on the other side of the transaction is unlikely to have any idea that someone with inside information was involved,"[xlvi] writes law professor Peter J. Henning. "The real victim is the market, a faceless mass of billions of dollars' worth of transactions daily."[xlvii] Once again, Wall Street must speak out much more forcefully against the practice of insider trading, telling its own to "knock it off; you are hurting us all."

Bubble Formula

There is one other promising, yet far less utilized, avenue available for prosecutors to pursue criminal prosecutions against top financial executives. Frank Partnoy, a professor at the University of San Diego Law School, told CBS' "60 Minutes" that Sarbanes-Oxley provisions requiring CEOs and CFOs to attest to the accuracy of financial statements represents a powerful tool in prosecutors' arsenal.[xlviii] "I hope that it will be used. I think there clearly are instances where CEOs and CFOs . . . signed financial statements that said there were adequate controls and there weren't adequate controls,"[xlix] Partney said. "But I can't explain why it hasn't been used yet."[l]

The answer lies in the need to control the runaway complexity of financial instruments and apply stricter accounting standards. Mortgage-backed securities were being carried at unrealistic values on the balance sheets of many financial institutions. Hedge fund investor Jim Chanos has referred to this as the "bezzle" of the embezzlement of the 2007–08 period.[li]

Chanos explained to CNBC television: " . . . securitizations at banks and brokerages could not be sold to people like me, at prices that they were being carried on the books. And consequently they kept them on the books at inflated prices—which means profits were reported higher than they really were, which means bonuses were taken in cash out of these institutions in cash. In effect, those institutions were looted. No one has gotten to the crux and examined the accounting, the risk management. Who knew where these things were marked and why? We keep hearing that these things were too complex. Well, why don't you try it."[lii]

When storm clouds surfaced, the mortgage-backed market collapsed with stunning speed. Values were changing so fast that it was nearly impossible for even the most conscientious of executives to keep up from an accounting perspective. While the complexity of the underlying financial instruments is clearly hindering criminal financial prosecutions, the accounting issues and executive certifications identified by Mr. Chanos and Professor Partnoy in banks' prior regulatory filings offer prosecutors fertile grounds to pursue criminal actions.

The lack of accounting fraud prosecutions illustrates one of the additional barriers to effective regulation: self-interested behavior *beyond* Wall Street. When asset prices are appreciating, politicians and the public often show little interest in vigorous enforcement. The government has a vested interest in assets going up in value, because bull markets boost both tax receipts and political careers. When 401(k)s are rising, the investing public is often indifferent to compliance matters. This attitude only fuels unrealistic investor expectations. Even professional investors have proven to be consistently complacent.

In reality, there is no less fraud and deception during bull markets than in bear markets. Regulation requires leading from the front rather than following behind to clean up after the circus. Markets, therefore, need the same regulatory zeal when things appear rosiest and companies are reporting record earnings. Where was the scrutiny on the accounting valuation and treatment of subprime assets *before* the bubble collapsed?

That's why there must also be a place in markets for negative information and opinion. Voices of dissent are too often stifled by issuer intimidation and retaliation. Negative analysis is, in fact, an essential early warning system to limit the size of costly bubbles. This is the time when careful scrutiny can have the largest preventative impact.

Some say public company financial statements require renewed attention. After a string of aggressive prosecution of firms like Enron, Tyco, Worldcom and Adelphia in the early part of the last decade, accounting fraud cases have slowed to a trickle in recent years. Historically, these cases typically involved mischief like inflating revenues or improperly classifying expenditures. "If the government spent half the time trying to ferret out fraud at major companies that it does tracking pump-and-dump schemes,"[liii] said law professor Bill Black of the University of Missouri at Kansas City, "we might have been able to stop the financial crisis, or at least we'd have a fighting chance at stopping the next one."[liv]

However, investigating the accounting practices of large corporations is sensitive stuff. These companies are important job creators for local communities and enjoy considerable political influence with home-state politicians. Prosecutions can result in corporate bankruptcies with significant collateral damage to innocent employees, retired workers, communities, and shareholders.

While the SEC and other regulators deserve praise for the effectiveness of their insider trading prosecutions, the same regulatory aggressiveness should be applied to corporate financial statements— regardless of the perceived economic impact or political sensitivity.

"The biggest threat to the financial system is one we probably don't know yet,"[lv] wrote banking analyst Mike Mayo, who gained respect and notoriety for his early warnings about the sector. "It's out there right now, lurking like a spore colony, tucked in some hidden crevice in the finances of big banks but not yet disclosed to investors."

Just like Wall Street itself, regulators must also start thinking globally. Allowing exaggerated financial statements to inflate bubbles ultimately threatens the entire system.

Notes, Chapter 4

i Katherine Leary Alsdorf interview with the author.

ii Ibid.

iii Ibid.

iv Anastasiya Pocheptsova, Rosellina Ferraro, and Ajay T. Abraham, "The Effect of Mobile Phone Use on Prosocial Behavior. http://newsdesk.umd.edu/uniini/release.cfm?ArticleID=2615.

v Ibid.

vi John C. Bogle, "There Were Once Things One Just Didn't Do," The New York Times, March 16, 2012.

vii Joseph A. Giannone, "Merril, Morgan Stanley seen losing grip on rich," Reuters, March 29, 2012. http://www.reuters.com/article/2012/03/29/us-brokerages-marketshare-idUSBRE82S0T320120329.

viii Dr. Joseph E. Stiglitz remarks, The Economist online debate, February 23, 2010. http://www.economist.com/debate/days/view/471.

ix Remarks by Chairman Alan Greenspan to the Federal Reserve Bank of Chicago's Forty-first Annual Conference on Bank Structure, May 5, 2005. http://www.federalreserve.gov/boarddocs/speeches/2005/2005050 5/default.htm.

x Jose A. Lopez, "Regulatory Evaluation of Value-at-Risk Models," Economic Research Department Federal Reserve Bank of San Francisco, June 30, 1999. http://www.frbsf.org/econrsrch/workingp/wpjl99-06.pdf.

xi Ben Protess, "Corzine and MF Global Regulators Testify," DealBook, December 8, 2011. http://dealbook.nytimes.com/2011/12/08/a-remorseful-corzine-set-to-testify-before-congress/.

xii The Holy Bible, Job 32:9, (KJV).

xiii John Mauldin, "American Gridlock," Outside the Box, January 30, 2012. http://www.johnmauldin.com/outsidethebox/american-gridlock.

xiv Remarks by President Barak Obama on 21st Century Financial Regulatory Reform," June 17, 2009.

http://www.whitehouse.gov/the_press_office/Remarks-of-the-President-on-Regulatory-Reform.

xv The Holy Bible, Deuteronomy 25:15, (NIV).

xvi Jean Eaglesham and Steve Eder, "SEC Ups its Game to Identify Rogue Firms," *The Wall Street Journal*, December 27, 2011. http://online.wsj.com/article/SB1000142405297020368620457711 16752943871934.html.

xvii John Stossell, "Job Creators Fight Back," *Fox Business*, December 13, 2011. http://www.foxbusiness.com/on-air/stossel/blog/2011/12/13/job-creators-fight-back.

xviii Ibid.

xix David Benoit, "Jamie Dimon's Letter: The Highlights," *Deal Journal*, April 4, 2012. http://blogs.wsj.com/deals/2012/04/04/jamie-dimons-letter-the-highlights/.

xx Rachelle Younglai, "SEC chief has regrets over short-selling ban," *Reuters*, December 31, 2008. http://www.reuters.com/article/2008/12/31/us-sec-cox-interview-idUSTRE4BU3FL20081231.

xxi Ibid.

xxii Ann Woolner, "Wall Street's Ways Make Jury Selection Tricky," *Bloomberg*, February 3, 2011. http://www.bloomberg.com/news/2011-02-04/wall-street-s-ways-make-jury-selection-tricky-commentary-by-ann-woolner.html.

xxiii William K. Black, "'The only winning move is not to play'-the insanity of the regulatory race to the bottom," *New Economic Perspectives*, March 25, 2012. http://neweconomicperspectives.org/2012/03/the-only-winning-move-is-not-to-play-the-insanity-of-the-regulatory-race-to-the-bottom.html.

xxiv Ibid.

xxv Ibid.

xxvi Lisa Swan, "MF Global Customers Looking for Their Own Missing Money," *CompliancEX*, January 12, 2012. http://compliancesearch.com/compliancex/mf-global-customers-looking-for-their-own-missing-money/.

xxvii Broc Romanek, "The Case for the SEC's Self-Funding: House Financial Services Chair's Alleged Insider Trading," *TheCorporateCounsel.net*, February 10, 2012. http://www.thecorporatecounsel.net/Blog/2012/02/-corp-fins-common-financial.html.

xxviii Jesse Eisinger, "Needed: A Cure for a Severe Case of Trialphobia," *Pro Publica*, December 14, 2011, http://www.propublica.org/thetrade/item/needed-a-cure-for-a-severe-case-of-trialphobia.

xxix "25 People to Blame for the Financial Crisis," *Time Specials*, http://www.time.com/time/specials/packages/article/0,28804,1877 351_1877350_1877323,00.html.

xxx US Securities and Exchange Commission Press Release, "SEC Enforcement Division Produces Record Results in Safeguarding Investors and Markets," November 9, 2011. http://sec.gov/news/press/2011/2011-234.htm.

xxxi Chairwoman Mary S. Shapiro's Letter to the Honorable Jack Reed, Chairman, Subcommittee on Securities, Insurance and Banking, November 28, 2011. http://dealbook.nytimes.com/2011/12/05/s-e-c-seeks-more-power-but-does-it-need-it/#letter.

xxxii Ibid.

xxxiii Pam Martens, "If This is a Financial Fortress, Run for the Bunkers," *Wall Street on Parade*, June 6, 2012. http://wallstreetonparade.com/2012/06/jpmorgan-if-this-is-a-financial-fortress-run-for-the-bunkers/.

xxxiv John S. Baker, Jr. and Dale E. Bennett, "Measuring the Explosive Growth of Federal Crime Legislation," *The Federalist Society*. http://fedsoc.server326.com/Publications/practicegroupnewsletter s/criminallaw/crimreportfinal.pdf.

xxxv Ibid.

xxxvi Ibid.

xxxvii "Criminal Prosecutions for Financial Institution Fraud Continue to Fall," *TRAC Reports*, November 15, 2011. http://trac.syr.edu/tracreports/crim/267/.

xxxviii Barack Obama, *The Audacity of Hope* (New York: Crown Publishers, 2006), 217.

xxxix Ben Protess, "For Wall Street Watchdog, All Grunt Work, Little Glory," *DealBook*, December 1, 2011. http://dealbook.nytimes.com/2011/12/01/for-wall-street-watchdog-all-grunt-work-little-glory/.

xl Patricia Hurtado, "FBI Pulls Off 'Perfect Hedge' to Nab New Insider Trading Class," Bloomberg, December 19, 2011. http://www.bloomberg.com/news/2011-12-20/fbi-pulls-off-perfect-hedge-to-nab-new-insider-trading-class.html.

xli Michael Rothfeld and Reed Albergotti, "U.S v Gupta: The Wiretaps," *The Wall Street Journal*, May 11, 2012. http://online.wsj.com/article/SB1000142405270230407030457396573418502132.html.

xlii Peter Lattman and Azam Ahmed, "Rajat Gupta Convicted of Insider Trading," *The New York Times*, June 15, 2012. http://dealbook.nytimes.com/2012/06/15/rajat-gupta-convicted-of-insider-trading/?nl=business&emc=edit_dlbkpm_20120615.

xliii Joel M. Cohen, Mary Kay Dunning, and Gregory H. Shill, "Erosion of the Fiduciary-Duty Requirement in Insider-Trading Actions," *American Bar Association Securities Litigation Journal*, Spring 2010. http://www.gibsondunn.com/publications/Documents/Cohen-Dunning-Shill-Fiduciary-Duty.pdf.

xliv Mathew Goldstein, "Steve Cohen says insider trading rules are 'vague,'" Reuters, December 13, 2011. http://www.reuters.com/article/2011/12/13/us-sac-cohen-deposition-idUSTRE7BC1UJ20111213.

xlv Ibid.

xlvi Peter J. Henning, "Insider trading riddle: Why do the rich risk it?," *The New York Times DealBook*, April 4, 2012. http://dealbook.nytimes.com/2012/04/04/insider-trading-riddle-why-do-the-rich-risk-it/.

xlvii Ibid.

xlviii Steve Kroft, "Prosecuting Wall Street," *60 Minutes*, December 4, 2011.

xlix Ibid.

l Ibid.

li Jim Chanos interview with CNBC Squawk Box, December 9, 2011.

lii Ibid.

liii David Weidner, "Why No Jail Time for Wall Street CEO's," *MarketWatch*, June 1, 2011.
http://articles.marketwatch.com/2011-05-31/commentary/30807731_1_financial-crisis-inquiry-commission-prosecutions-jail-time.

liv Ibid.

lv Mike Mayo, *Exile on Wall Street: One Analyst's Fight to Save the Big Banks From Themselves* (Hoboken: John Wiley & Sons, 2012), Kindle 3068.

5 Curb Appeal

Americans have always been an aspirational, socially mobile people, free to move up or down the ladder of economic success. Ever since our nation's founding, neither wealth nor poverty has ever been considered a permanent state. Think Horatio Alger.

The Founders believed deeply in equality of opportunity, rather than equality of outcomes. So, nearly a century later, did Abraham Lincoln, who said, "Property is the fruit of labor . . . property is desirable . . . is a positive good in the world. That some should be rich shows that others may become rich, and hence is just encouragement to industry and enterprise."[i]

Today, the traditional view of America as the Land of Opportunity and upward social mobility is being challenged. The recent financial crisis triggered an intense debate about fairness in America. Does everyone still have a chance to "make it big"? An October 2011 New York Times poll found that 67 percent of Americans still believed it was possible to start out poor in America and become rich,[ii] although that was down significantly from its February 2000 peak of 84 percent.[iii]

"Let Them Eat Cake"

There was a growing sense in the country that the financial system was rigged against the little guy. Against this backdrop, executive compensation became a hot-button issue, triggering a wave of populist anger and disgust against extravagant pay packages at companies receiving taxpayer-subsidized bailout funds.

By the time the financial crisis had largely passed, it left a path of destruction that included 8.8 million American job losses and five million foreclosures.[iv]   Main Street America was hurting, trying to shake off a giant economic hangover. Rising food, energy, health care and education costs further pressured living standards. Yet, financial executives seemed oblivious to how unfair their compensation packages appeared to those outside the industry.

The compensation outrage was not limited to this country, drawing world-wide condemnation.   For example, British Prime Minister David Cameron commented that the tone-deaf pay packages in the United Kingdom's bailed-out banking sector "made people's blood boil."[v]

Needless to say, the financial industry's compensation practices were a public relations disaster. *The New York Times'* Nicholas Kristoff outlined the potentially lasting damage, writing, "In the postwar years, labor unions became greedy and rewarded themselves with featherbedding and rigid work rules—turning much of the public against them. Likewise, Wall Street featherbedding is tarnishing the public image of banks and business and undermining confidence in capitalism itself."[vi]

The backlash was understandable given the widening wealth gap. Incomes for the top 1 percent of taxpayers rose by 30 percent from 2002 to 2008 while many Americans were struggling mightily.[vii] For many, Wall Street became the face of the "1 percent" fairness divide.

In recent decades, finance has flexed its muscles within the US economy, prompting some to call for shrinking the industry's influence. The financial services industry contributed nearly 6 percent of US GDP in 2009 and provides 6 percent or more of state gross domestic product in nearly half the country.[viii] According to Harvard professor Dr. Benjamin Friedman, the finance sector accounted for 10 percent of all profits earned by US corporations from the 1950s to the 1980s.[ix] In the first half of the last decade, financial profits reached 34 percent.[x]

Fueled by deregulation, the financial industry's representation among top income earners rose from 11 percent in 1979 to 18 percent by 2005.[xi] In contrast, the share of other professions among top earners, such as doctors (16 percent) and lawyers (8 percent), remained relatively unchanged over the same interval.[xii]

While outsourcing, enhanced productivity tools and globalization held back wages in many sectors of the American economy, wage differentials for Wall Street professionals exploded relative to workers in other fields. By 2009, employees in the securities and investments sector, which includes investment banks, securities brokerages and commodities dealers, earned 3.4 times as much as the average US worker (versus 1.5 times the average non-farm US worker in 1929).[xiii] According to research from NYU's Thomas Philippon and the University of Virginia's Ariell Reshef, bonuses and salaries in finance increased 70 percent more than average pay in other industries between 1980 and 2005.[xiv]

To make matters worse, the big Wall Street banks even stood out like the proverbial sore thumb within the broader financial industry. "The average 2009 investment banking compensation at four of the top banks was at least six times that of an average American worker—while employees in the traditional commercial bank sector earned just 1.2 times the average non-farm employee,"[xv] wrote Robert G. Wilmers, chief executive officer of M&T Bank Corp., a mid-sized regional bank.

The numbers looked even more striking at the top of the biggest corporations, said Mr. Wilmers. The CEOs of the six largest bank holding companies were paid 2.3 times the average total CEO compensation of the top Fortune 50 nonbank companies—outlandish even by CEO standards.[xvi] At the same time, other analysis found that bank heads showed the greatest disconnect with their shareholders' performance during that time, with half of them garnering raises despite flagging stock prices.[xvii]

Executive perks and status symbols were nothing new on Wall Street. Box seats for New York Rangers' games had long been a hot item. Hermes ties, with the classic carriage label on the back and the distinctive "H" pattern on the front, were a familiar part of Wall Street's standard banker uniform.

During the housing bubble, though, Wall Street acted like the US had entered a new Gilded Age. Outsized wealth and power fueled even more ostentatious forms of status and conspicuous consumption. This included an insatiable appetite for luxury real estate, and such over-the-top extravagances as a million-dollar fantasy football league exclusive to high-powered financiers.[xviii] Increasingly, Wall Street saw the growing inequality as a sign of meritocracy, justifying the spoils as the product of superior skill and intellect.

When asset prices were rising, there were few voices of protest. Both New York City and New York State rely heavily on the tax receipts of the very same people who helped to cause the financial crisis. The financial industry accounted for 16.4 percent of New York's overall state GDP in 2008.[xix] In a competitive marketplace of global financial centers, there was always the specter of losing American financial jobs and functions to non-US jurisdictions like London, Switzerland or Hong Kong. In the words of writer Peggy Noonan, "You know you have to preserve them just when you'd most like to deck them."[xx]

When financial markets fell into crisis, critics said the excesses signaled an obvious detachment from broader society, and the public thought Wall Street was profiting at their expense. Sensitive to that anger, official Washington imposed limits on how much banks that received TARP bailout funds could pay out in compensation. However, those limits were short-lived, because most of the banks hastened to repay their TARP loans, whereupon they quickly reverted to their old ways and reinstated lavish pay packages. The financial community once again missed an opportunity to demonstrate sound judgment and sensitivity to the public's mood.

Banking analyst Mike Mayo identified Wall Street internal income inequalities: "Wall Street has its own 99 percent and 1 percent,"[xxi] he explained. "The 1 percent continues to win against the 99 percent."[xxii] The chief executive officers at the top six bank holding companies were paid an average of $26 million in 2007, or 516 times the US median household income.[xxiii]

Just as there is a divide between Wall Street and Main Street, so there is a wide economic gap between Wall Street's top executives and the financial industry's rank-and-file workers. According to a study by the City University of New York's Center for Urban Research, the median compensation for a white man in the New York financial industry between 2005 and 2009 was $154,500 (significantly less for women and minority workers).[xxiv]

With incomes like that, most financial professionals certainly don't qualify as hardship cases. Many had ample safety nets to weather the financial crisis, unlike millions of other Americans. But Wall

Street's "working class" has been the hardest hit by painful rounds of workforce reductions. The banking industry alone, for example, shed an estimated 230,000 jobs in 2011.[xxv] Included among them were many of the nation's 7,400 smaller banks and savings institutions, distributing the pain far beyond New York's financial district.[xxvi]

There is much to be learned from studying compensation issues in the run-up to and during the financial crisis itself. As was so often the case, a leadership failure was an essential ingredient. Wall Street's pay structures distorted incentives and fueled the credit crisis. Exorbitant compensation packages fed the ambition, hubris and greed that, in turn, promoted the excessive risk-taking that pushed Wall Street beyond prudent risk parameters. It is also a reminder of the dangers of complexity for the sake of complexity and the need for real innovation. Finally, some of Wall Street's attitudes toward compensation can be found embedded in broader American society.

For all these reasons, compensation issues serve as the CliffsNotes of the financial crisis. Compensation reform then offers a prototype for addressing many of the financial system's major excesses. Meaningful reform will have to be multifaceted. We propose a three-legged stool: judicious regulation, market solutions, and higher ethical standards.

The First Leg: Regulatory Solutions

As James Madison, our fourth president, noted, "If men were angels, no government would be necessary."[xxvii] It would be easier for all concerned if the discipline of market competition and an internal ethical code prevented financial professionals from violating trusts and committing mischief, but that has proven insufficient, and so we must "suffer it to be so now" and accept the need for additional governmental regulatory oversight.

In some cases, Wall Street misbehavior has been deliberate, in other cases, accidental; in many cases, though, the problem has been structural flaws in the system. As Mervynn King, governor of the Bank of England, put it, "the majority in the industry are good men and women. It is a matter of the incentives they face."[xxviii]

Incentives change behavior, and in the case of the financial industry, that behavior, such as basing bank employee pay on the volume of mortgage applications, was destructive. Because Wall Street could not restrain itself from designing inappropriate incentives, it invited additional regulation. The most prominent of these was the Wall Street Reform and Consumer Protection Act of 2010 (Dodd-Frank), the impact of which would be felt far beyond the financial services industry.

One of the more controversial provisions is Section 953(b) of the Dodd-Frank Act, a rule still being fine-tuned by the US Securities and Exchange Commission. The rule requires companies to calculate and disclose the ratio of the total annual compensation of the chief executive officer to the median annual total compensation of all other employees.

At a conceptual level, the ratio is easy to understand and appeals to basic fairness instincts. Management guru Peter Drucker, for example, often urged his CEO clients not to exceed a 20-to-1 salary ratio within their companies.[xxix]

Section 953(b) provides an important reminder that the failure to self-regulate invites blunt, heavy-handed regulation. The pay ratio is the equivalent of the compensation "Scarlet Letter," and it is entirely industry–self-inflicted.

Many large multinational corporations have protested that tabulating all the relevant data to calculate these ratios will be too costly and time-consuming in exchange for minimal benefits to investors. They cite the complications caused by option awards, deferred compensation, changes in pension values, etc.

It appears, though, that the SEC has some regulatory flexibility on the calculation issue. Since the statute is silent on the term "median," the SEC likely can permit companies to use statistical sampling (a subset) of their employee population to determine the median.[xxx] Others say even sampling is prohibitive since larger multinational companies do not maintain a centralized list of employees that is linked to their compensation information.[xxxi] While sampling may still be prohibitive for some companies, there is likely a workable compromise solution to reduce the data collection burden.

The real question is the value to the investor. Some, such as the AFL-CIO Office of Investment, argue that the pay ratio allows employees to easily compare their personal pay to the firm's CEO.[xxxii] A stronger argument is that the ratio gives outside shareholders a rare glimpse into worker satisfaction via median employee pay calculations.[xxxiii] Companies are also free to enhance their Section 953(b) disclosures with additional explanatory narrative,[xxxiv] thereby somewhat reducing the risk of negative stigmas.

However, the pay ratio is, at best, an imprecise measure and prone to efforts to massage the data. It is largely a punitive provision of little actionable or material value for investors and therefore should be overhauled. In short, the headline-grabbing pay-ratio gambit diverts attention and energy from potentially more worthwhile, effective regulations.

A more promising provision of Dodd-Frank is Section 954— "Erroneously Awarded Compensation." Its purpose is to better align compensation with performance by requiring listed companies to "claw back" (recover) from current or former executive officers any compensation they have received as a result of manipulating earnings. Section 954 is designed to prevent executives from personally profiting from fictitious paper profits that must later be restated. This section of Dodd-Frank expands upon the Sarbanes-Oxley Act's provisions authorizing the SEC to recoup incentive compensation from CEOs and CFOs who have engaged in financial reporting misconduct.

Preliminary research indicates that early adoption of clawback policies gives a short-term performance boost to firms.[xxxv] Clawbacks are popular with shareholders, not only because of the obvious justice of making the guilty pay, but also because these policies can induce better executive decisions by reducing timing mismatches—that is, rewarding executives today for managerial decisions when the actual consequences of those decisions won't become apparent until months or years later.[xxxvi]

By 2011, almost 70 percent of S&P 500 firms had adopted some sort of clawback policy.[xxxvii] While these provisions have been around for several years, boards of directors rarely exercised their forfeiture powers to take back some or all of employee bonuses. Therefore, some activist shareholders urged Wall Street firms to further strengthen and expand the use of their clawback authority.

As a result, many financial firms added extra teeth to existing clawback provisions in the wake of the credit crisis. These additional provisions allow firms to recover prior bonus payments from employees (and sometimes their managers) who engage in conduct that damages financial statements or results in legal or reputational harm. Under these expanded clawbacks, rogue traders, for example, are made to share the pain of unauthorized trades or improper risk-taking.

Also under expanded powers granted under Dodd-Frank, Federal Deposit Insurance Corp. (FDIC) regulators will be able to recover some of the pay of top US financial executives if a bank fails and is subsequently liquidated by the government.[xxxviii] Finally, new global banking regulations from the Basel Committee on Banking Supervision are expected to require financial firms to disclose aggregate dollar amounts clawed back in a given year.[xxxix]

Clawback provisions are only useful if they are regularly and consistently employed. Any attempt to push Wall Street to better police itself is progress. So are mechanisms that hold management and boards more directly accountable for reckless actions that shift the burden to taxpayers.

Besides the clawback provision, another constructive plank in Dodd-Frank is Section 955, which expands the scope of required company disclosures surrounding employee and director hedging practices. This provision came in response to public frustration with Wall Street executives' ability to profit under any circumstances, a "heads they win, tails they win" set of outcomes.

Most people don't begrudge a capitalistic system in which top executives are rewarded for their companies' successes, but they feel it is unjust for them to be rewarded for failure. What people oppose is a system that offers executives a "heads they win, tails they win" set of outcomes. In the words of Dr. Vince Cable, the business secretary in Britain's coalition cabinet, "What is completely unacceptable is that we have rewards for failure. We have extreme pay unrelated to performance. I want to see responsible capitalism."[xl]

In response to public pressure, corporate boards are emphasizing pay-for-performance in designing compensation policies. When implemented, Section 955 will likely cause firms to adopt a formal hedging policy, something that has been missing in many companies. Some companies may ban the practice of hedging altogether. Either way, shareholders benefit by understanding how a company allows its officers, directors and employees to shield themselves from poor company performance.

Indeed, hedging is a troublesome practice. Its defenders point out that hedging techniques provide their holders with diversification benefits, but they overlook the twofold downside of hedging. First, many hedges involve complex derivatives that lack transparency. In addition, these instruments are specifically designed to protect executives, directors or employees from a decline in the value of a company's stock, thereby misaligning interests with shareholders and running counter to the intent of pay-for-performance by insulating company personnel from any negative impact of their own policies.

Pay-for-performance compensation, while ethically superior to guaranteed riches regardless of performance, has its own fairness challenges. Designing effective incentives requires more thought than simply tying executive compensation to a rising stock price. Peeling back the layers of this problem helps both to better understand why the financial crisis occurred and what can be done to prevent it from happening again.

Under pressure from regulators, banks began doling out generous restricted stock and option awards to top executives, rather than cash, in the years following the financial crisis. It became common for firms to defer some or all of bonus payments to its high-level executives. The policy was designed, in theory, to reduce the temptation to "swing for the fences" in the short run while also softening the short-term impact of compensation expenses on a bank's financial statements.

Restricted stock is attractive to holders since, unlike stock options, shares aren't subject to the risk that the stock price can sink below the grant price. Both restricted stock and option awards granted when stock prices are deeply depressed, such as in 2008–2010, offer executives a potentially large windfall when markets recover.

With deferred stock, for example, the lower the firm's stock price, the more shares an employee can receive. One banker anonymously told *The New York Times* in late 2011 that he "prayed" every day that his firm's stock price did not go up before bonuses were handed out in early 2012, claiming that it was "all anyone is thinking about."[xli]

A stock option entitles its owner to buy a share of company stock at a set price over a specified period, attempting to align the executive's interest with those of the shareholders. At the same time, companies can claim a tax deduction in future years upon the executive's exercise for any appreciation beyond the fair market value expense of the options at the date of grant.[xlii]

When markets staged an impressive multi-year, 100 percent-plus recovery rally beginning in March of 2009, those who had received shares or share options during the preceding market turndown were well positioned to reap the rewards. This raises an important question: How much of a firm's stock price appreciation was due to executive acumen (performance) and how much was produced by hitching a free ride on a deeply oversold, broad market rally fueled by ultra-easy Federal Reserve monetary policy?

In 2011, for example, all stocks seemed to move together. "It was as if every S&P 500 company had the same chairman of the board that knew only one strategy, resulting in a high degree of correlation between seemingly unrelated companies,"[xliii] declared bond market expert Jim Bianco.

"These options gave executives a highly leveraged bet that stock prices would rebound from their 2008 and 2009 lows, and are now rewarding them for rising tides rather than performance,"[xliv] said Robert J. Jackson Jr., an associate professor of law at Columbia. "The tax code does nothing to ensure that these rewards go only to executives who have created sustainable long-term value."[xlv]

Some question the entire premise that stock-based compensation truly aligns executives with shareholders or improves actual operating performance. They argue that top executives should be paid solely in cash compensation, reducing CEOs' temptation to continually goose stock prices. "So the primary incentive at all times for executives with heavy stock-based compensation is to increase expectations—even when expectations are so high they can never be met,"[xlvi] wrote Roger Martin, dean of the Joseph L. Rotman School of Management at the University of Toronto. "Because expectations take into account everything that investors now understand, the only way to increase expectations from the current level is to positively surprise investors—to produce results better than they couldn't have expected."[xlvii]

That is why, Martin says, bank executives turned to the creation of exotic derivatives and proprietary trading.[xlviii] They could no longer exceed analyst and investor expectations, i.e., positively surprise, with staid traditional banking services. With the repeal of the 1933 Glass-Steagall Act, legislation that separated investment banking from commercial banking, new hybrid FDIC-insured financial institutions could push the envelope. Therefore, greater leverage was increasingly applied to risky strategies—juicing profits in the early years and yielding record compensation, but ultimately ending very badly for long-term shareholders and employees.

To prevent another financial system meltdown, former Fed Chairman Paul Volcker proposed the so-called "Volcker Rule," which would ban proprietary trading at financial firms that enjoy a government backstop. There is no more controversial and deeply-opposed provision of Dodd-Frank than the Volcker rule.

While the proposed rule does not go into effect until 2014, its implementation would forever alter the profit potential and "expectations" envelope for many of the nation's largest financial depositary institutions. That's why banks have hired an army of lobbyists to fight the rule at every turn.

In fairness, the Volcker Rule does complicate issues for global capital markets, although not in any insurmountable way. Wall Street banks say the rule will limit their ability to provide liquidity to the financial markets. The large banks act as "market makers," holding ample inventories of stocks, bonds or other instruments at the ready on behalf of their clients, matching buyers and sellers for a middleman's fee. Also, banks claim that if they can't make their own proprietary bets, it will further reduce liquidity and thereby drive up the costs for all other market participants.

A number of foreign governments and their regulators have even lobbied Congress to carve out loopholes to exempt sovereign government bonds from the rule. If large banks can't buy, for example, significant quantities of foreign debt, ostensibly to satisfy anticipated customer demand, it will drive up the borrowing costs of deeply indebted foreign governments. Many corporate debt issuers have made a similar argument. So has Uncle Sam. In fact (and this probably won't surprise you) US government debt is the one asset already exempt from the proposed Volcker Rule.

There is often a very fine line between essential market-making and speculative proprietary trading, though. When a bank buys high-yielding Greek government bonds, for example, it takes them onto its balance sheet. While it waits to execute trades, customer demand could dry up or the bonds could decline in value if the Greek government restructures its debts, for example. This type of scenario occurred during the financial crisis. Banks were stuck with toxic mortgage securities when customer demand evaporated.

Sometimes, though, banks buy Greek bonds, betting that the value of those same Greek bonds will go up. In other words, their motive is not to make a market, but to make a buck by reaping a trading profit from its inventory. Banks argue that it would be impossible for regulators to determine their intent, and that by banning the practice of holding excess inventory, the regulation would kill off essential market-making.

Mr. Volcker himself rebutted that argument, responding, "Holding substantial securities in a trading book for an extended period obviously assumes the character of a proprietary position, particularly if not specifically hedged."[xlix] The rule aims to prevent banks from masking proprietary trading as market-making. The fact that banks can cloak their risky activities shows why regulation is appropriate and necessary.

Indeed, the Volcker Rule isn't perfect. There are loopholes and many questions, like how to handle odd-lot (or non-standard unit) transactions on behalf of clients. There will be considerable compliance costs too. Nor can proprietary trading be blamed for bad underwriting standards that fueled the housing bubble. Banks also lose money making bad loans, yet, no one is calling for banks to similarly stop making loans.

But the banks' claim that the Volcker Rule would jeopardize market-making is disingenuous. Market-making is a profitable business. If large banks choose to exit this profitable activity, smaller nonbank players will quickly take their place. Inventories of corporate and mortgage-backed bonds at large banks have already fallen because of stricter capital requirements, not because of the Volcker Rule.

As for any claim that regulators are trying to shut down banks' proprietary trading operations, that, too, isn't a valid argument. Banks could spin off such operations into an independent business entity that wouldn't be eligible to receive federal bailouts.

For all the teeth-gnashing over the Volcker Rule, it's important to not forget from where we recently came. Former Citigroup Chairman Richard Parsons told *Bloomberg Businessweek* in 2011 that if Citi had been allowed to fail by the government, "You wouldn't be able to buy a loaf of bread or clear a check. It would be like Egypt. People would be out on the streets."[l] Leading banking analysts concluded that twelve of the thirteen largest US banks would have failed without government intervention.[li] Given the role that proprietary trading activities played in making the financial crisis as severe as it was, particularly by distorting incentives, are we willing to risk a repeat? The Volcker Rule makes sense.

Consider what happened in the spring of 2012, four years after the crisis' darkest hours. J.P. Morgan surprised markets by disclosing that it had lost an estimated $4-$5 billion in synthetic credit derivatives bets on US corporate bonds. While trading from its CIO's office typically accounts for a small portion of company earnings, J.P. Morgan CEO Jamie Dimon conceded that the revelation "plays right into the hands of a whole bunch of pundits out there,"[lii] and will make it harder to lobby against the Volcker Rule. One of those "pundits," Frank Partnoy, a professor of law and finance at the University of San Diego, declared, "It couldn't have come at a worse time for JPMorgan Chase. After everything we went through in the financial crisis, the fact that something of this magnitude could happen shows that the reform didn't do the job."[liii]

Mr. Dimon, respected as one of the most skilled CEOs in the banking sector, frankly admitted that internal traders had made "egregious"[liv] errors. In a conference call with analysts, he admitted, "In hindsight, the strategy was flawed, complex, poorly reviewed, poorly executed and poorly monitored."[lv]   In subsequent congressional testimony, Jamie Dimon suggested that J.P. Morgan was contemplating invoking its "clawback" provisions to recover pay from those who may have misled him or other senior managers.[lvi]

The fact that the derivatives problem could have occurred at J.P. Morgan, the one large bank generally thought to have largely sidestepped most of the financial crisis through shrewd management, plainly illustrates much of the underlying problem. "But in his hubris, Dimon was never willing to acknowledge that just because he had sidestepped yesterday's problems didn't mean he was going to sidestep tomorrow's,"[lvii] wrote *The New York Times*' Joe Nocera. While Mr. Dimon told analysts that the losses would not have run afoul of Dodd-Frank, many were left saying, "If this could happen at J.P. Morgan, imagine what could happen elsewhere."

In truth, all the major banks engage in similar credit derivatives trading. It is not currently prohibited. Banks make loans that comprise a credit portfolio. They also often trade credit default swaps (or insurance-like derivatives) *against* those same loans, calling it "portfolio hedging." Special situation hedge funds typically take the other side of these trades. These instruments are "synthetic" in that they do not actually include the underlying corporate bonds but rather are a derivative index designed to move with the corporate credits, a derivative of a derivative. If a financial institution becomes too large of a player in certain segments of the derivatives market, it can "become the market." In that case, the bank is trapped—too large to effectively hedge the underlying assets or unwind its derivatives position in the event of adverse conditions.

Historically, banks have always hedged their interest rate risk. Dodd-Frank specifically permits banks to hedge positions in both their market-making activities and investment portfolios. It's not always clear, though, whether the trading is being done to hedge exposure to events like an economic downturn or to generate additional investment income for the bank—a legitimate hedge or an outright bet? J.P. Morgan's revelation that it had suffered large losses by *selling* derivative protection against its bond portfolio left many scratching their heads. "Selling protection is effectively the same as buying more bonds,"[lviii] wrote *The New York Times*' Peter Eavis. "If the bonds go down in value, so will the sold protection. So how can that be a hedge, investors might have asked?"

Three things are clear about this type of derivatives trading: Sometimes the hedges go awry, there can be embedded conflicts of interest, and it is often a very profitable business.

Banks could simply elect to sell some of the underlying assets rather than engage in exotic hedges on them. But large financial institutions can't generate significant profit growth from their core retail banking business, and artificially low interest rates have taken a large bite out of the fee revenue from their broker-dealer arms. At the same time, the front end of the yield curve is so flat due to Federal Reserve policy that banks can't profitably borrow short and lend longer as they have traditionally done.

So, Wall Street banks turn to proprietary and credit book trading to boost profits and bonuses. If a bank's "go-to" move to get through any tough operating environment is simply to add more leverage to these investment activities, is it any wonder why Wall Street took its eye off culture and values issues? A company's broader culture and values are irrelevant to this type of activity. All you need is a small band of fearless traders, a big balance sheet to support the leverage, and a risk model to convince regulators that you know what you are doing.

Figuring out ways to minimize the risk of large FDIC-insured banks taking outsized bets at taxpayer expense is of crucial importance. A repeat of the 2008 meltdown is still possible because of Wall Street's current approach to risk and reward. Gone are the partnership days, and in its place the Street is dominated by global multinational corporations with 25,000-50,000 employees and a small number of top executives garnering the bulk of the rewards.

The partnership model was an example of "owners' capitalism," where those who put up their own capital bore the attendant risks. If they were right, they reaped the rewards; if wrong, it was their own money that was lost. That old model has been replaced by a "corporate managers' capitalism" that risks primarily shareholders' capital. It is the equivalent of playing the game with someone else's money. Going one step further, when firms are supported by an implicit taxpayer-funded backstop, it is akin to also playing with the house's money.

While there is ample evidence that top executives of Wall Street firms experienced significant reductions in their personal wealth (via aggregate stock and option holdings) as a result of the financial crisis,[lix] they weren't the kind of life-altering losses that serve as a powerful deterrent.

Meaningful personal capital at risk has proven to be a powerful curb on reckless behavior. Warren Buffet said of those large bank executives who allowed and encouraged reckless risk-taking, "You should go broke, and I think your wife should go broke too."[lx]

Professor and author Nassim Taleb also identified inherent agency problems in the managers' capitalism system. "The potency of my solution lies in the idea that people do not consciously wish to harm themselves; I feel much safer on a plane because the pilot, and not a drone, is at the controls,"[lxi] wrote Taleb. "Similarly, cooks should taste their own cooking; engineers should stand under the bridges they have designed when the bridges are tested; the captain should be the last to leave the ship."[lxii]

In fact, that is the way it works in the hedge fund space, where industry practice demands that hedge fund managers invest the large majority of their liquid personal wealth in their own funds. Such a demonstration of commitment by the manager is a standard due-diligence requirement for most institutions contemplating an allocation. Investors want to see that the manager will suffer the greatest personal pain in the event of a blowup.

This form of discipline helps to explain why no hedge fund required a federal bailout during the financial crisis—even though hedge funds were also subject to many of the very same stresses that nearly cratered other segments of the financial industry.

As it specifically relates to compensation and proprietary trading, there are indeed elements of Dodd-Frank that are worth preserving and embracing. In other areas of Dodd-Frank, a lighter regulatory hand is required. Trading is not immoral, and there is no way to regulate risk from capital markets. But managers' capitalism and too-big-to-fail banks are a dangerous brew that is still being bottled in America's largest banks.

The existence of such profound moral hazards necessitates proper regulatory constraint. As Nassim Taleb succinctly summarized, "Bonuses and bailouts should never mix."[lxiii]

The Second Leg: Market Solutions

Ill-conceived and designed incentive systems do more to pervert capitalism than perhaps any other influence. Regulation alone isn't flexible enough to keep up with dynamic, highly specialized global capital markets. Self-regulating market forces are also needed to rein in excesses and restore balance.

Like most issues surrounding the financial crisis, runaway executive compensation is not unique to Wall Street. Executive compensation in general is broken. CEOs across all industries, not just financial services, have been consistently getting 10-15 percent raises a year while their own middle managers hope for 2-3 percent increases. Unless a corporation's profit rises 10-15 percent annually, giving CEOS perennial raises of that magnitude is economically unsustainable and ethically indefensible.

According to the Institute for Policy Studies, CEOs at large US firms raked in a 28 percent annual increase in 2010, receiving, on average, $10.8 million, while the average worker saw his pay increase by a mere 3 percent, to $33,121.[lxiv] In 1980, CEOs of large US companies received an average of $624,996 in annual compensation, or 42 times the pay of their employees.[lxv] By 2010, CEO compensation had ballooned to 319 times the median worker's pay.[lxvi]

Amid the growing chorus of public outcry, Dodd-Frank aimed to give shareholders more of a voice on executive pay. The act mandated public companies to provide their shareholders with an advisory vote on executive compensation, known as "say-on-pay" votes.

At most publicly traded companies, the compensation committee of the board of directors is tasked with determining CEO pay. Under the new rules, boards must put their executive pay packages to a non-binding shareholder vote at least once every three years.

Britain installed similar non-binding shareholder votes on executive pay several years earlier. However, the provisions did little to check the escalation of UK executive compensation. British boards of directors were as generous as their American counterparts, typically awarding a 3 percent increase in chief executive's pay per 10 percent increase in a firm's market value.[lxvii] In contrast, average workers' pay gained only 0.2 percent with the same market value growth, according to the London School of Economics.[lxviii] British Minister David Cameron has said that he favors giving shareholders a binding vote in the largest companies, vowing to "redefine the word 'fair.'"[lxix]

The early results of the American "say-on-pay" experiment closely resembled those of the British experiment. US investors initially appeared remarkably indifferent to having their newfound "say." In 2011, the first year US Dodd-Frank universal "say-on-pay" rules first went into effect, shareholder attitudes looked very similar to those before enactment. Based on proxy research firm ISS data, an average of 92 percent of votes was cast in favor of company executive compensation proposals.[lxx] Only forty-two out of more than three thousand companies failed to achieve majority support.[lxxi] According to a Council of Institutional Investors study, investors delivered a majority "no" vote rebuke on proposed executive compensation less than 2 percent of the time during the 2011 proxy season.[lxxii]

The reality is that investors have traditionally rubber-stamped executive compensation practices, dutifully accepting management's recommendation. In recent years, individual investors have increasingly failed to make their voices heard on executive compensation policies. In the 1970s, individual investors exercised their proxy vote about 74 percent of time.[lxxiii] Today, as few as 10 percent of individual shareholders are casting their proxy votes in time for corporate annual meetings.[lxxiv]

While research from professors Alexandra Niessen and Camelia Kuhnen found that firms do react to public outcry over compensation policies,[lxxv] many small investors believe their votes don't matter or find the entire proxy voting process too confusing. In part, the attitude reflects the fact that most Americans now own shares through mutual funds and other pooled vehicles. Ninety million Americans or 44 percent of the nation's households owned mutual funds in 2010.[lxxvi] In contrast, individual investors owned 94 percent of all stocks in 1950 and 63 percent of equities in 1980.[lxxvii] By 2008, that number had fallen to 34 percent.[lxxviii]

Individual shareholders mistakenly believe that their investment managers are monitoring executive pay on their behalf as part of the stock selection process. Under proxy voting rules, institutional investors vote large blocks of shares on behalf of their many individual investors. Proxy voting is the primary means by which shareholders can influence a company's operations and policies. However, institutional asset managers are often reluctant to collect the necessary information to analyze executive compensation[lxxix] and therefore fail to exert their considerable clout in this area. Many view voting proxies as a "check-the-box" compliance requirement rather than a part of their investment selection process.

"The persons who make buy-and-sell decisions, institutional and retail, don't really care about voting their shares except on matters of clear economic significance to them as owners of equity,"[lxxx] wrote Charles M. Nathan and Parul Mehta of the law firm Latham and Watkins, " . . . our current structure of annual shareholder meetings and a plethora of shareholder proposals is simply not interesting or relevant to the vast majority of investment decision makers."[lxxxi]

Because of the sheer number of voting decisions faced by institutional shareholders, standard industry practice is to delegate voting decisions to internal or external governance specialists.[lxxxii] As a result, there is a discontinuity between institutional managers who make portfolio management decisions and those who make the decisions on how to vote portfolio shares on matters such as executive compensation.[lxxxiii]

In fairness, asset managers already face serious information overload. Just shy of 14,000 shareholder meetings were held by publicly traded companies in the US in 2010.[lxxxiv] It is a formidable challenge for busy investment managers to perform their essential day-to-day functions. Pressed for time, they count on third-party proxy advisory services to tell them how to vote on governance issues. Although not every large asset manager follows the recommendations of the proxy advisory firms in a lockstep manner, most rely heavily on their input.

As a result, institutional asset managers frequently apply formulaic one-size-fits-all voting policies across their portfolio companies.[lxxxv] The analysis typically involves a checklist of basic, largely qualitative measures such as years of experience of board members or whether the CEO and chairman are separate individuals. Knowing this, boards often tailor their compensation and governance policies to specifically adhere to the proxy advisory firms' metrics.

These same service providers also advise issuers on how to lobby their institutional shareholder base to obtain the necessary threshold of proxy votes. Potential conflict issues, therefore, must also be managed when advisory firms function in the dual role of both advising and rating firms on their corporate governance issues.

There are other reasons why professional managers don't adopt a more forceful approach to the compensation policies of their holdings. Some are concerned that company executives will engage in retribution if proxy solicitation firms can deduce that they voted against management's recommendations.[lxxxvi] Other managers are indifferent because they too are highly compensated individuals and are therefore not as sensitive to pay practices. Finally, some managers are themselves employees of public companies subject to "say-on-pay" provisions. They are reluctant to adopt an overtly activist approach to portfolio companies for fear that it may draw uncomfortable scrutiny of their *own* firm's senior executive team.

It's not the place of the asset management community to micromanage pay within corporations or second-guess every decision of a compensation committee, particularly without knowledge of a firm's internal dynamics. That's why it doesn't make much sense to give shareholders a fully binding say on pay. But the pendulum has simply swung too far the other way, with institutional investors being too deferential to corporate boards.

At present, most investment professionals know very little about the compensation polices of the companies they purchase on behalf of investors. They delegate the evaluation of compensation policies to "a parallel universe of voting decision makers."[lxxxvii] In so doing, they fail to exercise independent judgment or apply their own considerable analytical firepower and acumen to improve the design of executive compensation.

Some influential pension funds have demonstrated strong leadership in compensation reform. Others have banded together to seek governance changes.[lxxxviii] During the 2012 proxy season, more shareholders pushed back against proposed pay packages.

However, the great majority of institutional managers would rather simply sell their shares than try to understand or fix complicated corporate governance issues. They vote with their feet. That's because the average holding period for US investors has fallen to under seven months, down from the roughly seven-year average holding period from 1940 to 1975.[lxxxix]

Even if institutional investor attitudes could be changed about the relevance of compensation issues on share performance, a key ingredient would *still* be missing. While corporations have improved their proxy statement descriptions in response to Dodd-Frank, shareholders still lack the necessary tools to make informed decisions about complex compensation instruments that include pension contributions, deferred bonuses, and a custom blend of long-term incentives.

"People have to know what they are voting on,"[xc] says Dr. Carr Bettis, financial engineering expert and founder of research firm Incentive Lab. This dilemma illustrates one of the limitations of a strictly regulatory approach to financial reform. Regulators can mandate shareholder say-on-pay provisions. There is no way to decree *informed* voting, however.

The basic problem is that incentive programs have become so complex that they outstrip even sophisticated institutional shareholders' ability to understand them. "The simple truth is that remuneration schemes have become too complex and, in some cases, too generous and out of line with the interests of investors,"[xci] said Dominic Rossi of Fidelity Worldwide Investment. "Tell us in simple terms what you propose and let shareholders decide."[xcii] As we have already discussed, complexity without rigor is neither thoughtful nor effective. This fact applies as much to compensation design as it does to financial products.

Boards of directors aren't compensation experts. So, they turn to consultants to construct cutting-edge executive pay packages. Complexity is the compensation consultant's best friend, creating a lucrative market for his or her specialized expertise.

Peel back the layers of complexity on some of these sophisticated compensation plans and you find that they are often backed up by very little quantitative rigor. The designs are embraced largely because other companies are using them, leading to inadequate peer group benchmarking. Therefore, changing the construct of compensation requires a better understanding of firm-specific impacts.

The current tools available to boards, compensation consultants and investment managers to measure compensation outcomes are simply inadequate. Measurement of outcomes requires refined math, statistical, and modeling skills—typically not the purview of boards of directors or even most compensation consultants.

Like many other aspects of modern finance, compensation began evolving so rapidly with fierce competition for top talent that no one bothered to stop and ask, "Does this really work?" And more importantly, "Does it work for *this* company?"

Not all compensation plans are created equal. Consultants and boards of directors would benefit from measuring and monitoring which mix of so-called time-vested and performance-vested instruments (such as accounting metrics) truly delivers the best incentives for a given company and industry.

By solving the information vacuum, boards of directors could also more effectively negotiate pay packages for new CEO hires. Boards frequently overpay, justifying the new CEO package based on a need to attract scarce, seasoned executive talent, while often ignoring the impact on shareholder value or company culture.

However, the executive talent pool is not as thin as many boards would seem to think. Globally there are many talented people available who are not part of the narrow search consultant's network. Too much emphasis is given to legacy CEOs. This closed circle of recycled CEOs further inflates executive compensation.

"Greater scientific rigor produces better information—which results in improved decision making in the area of compensation design," explains Dr. Carr Bettis. A market-based ecosystem is, therefore, required to address the underlying problem of opaque compensation instruments that frustrate effective "say-on-pay." If individual investors demand that their investment managers more thoroughly and independently evaluate compensation policies, research and information providers like Bloomberg and Thomson Reuters will inevitably develop better tools to meet the requirements of their asset manager clients.

More powerful analytical tools will demonstrate to investment managers that the performance targets and peer firms used by boards of directors to set compensation policy do, in fact, directly impact company performance.

As watchdogs for shareholder interests, institutional investment managers will influence boards of directors to apply more thought, transparency and judgment to compensation policies. In response to these market-based pressures, corporate boards will then continually refine compensation policies and commit to clearer explanations.

This is an example of a new engagement model—one where individual investors, Wall Street's asset managers, and boards of directors are each thrust into the role of guardian of the capitalist system. The bottom line is: While "say on pay" regulations may arm shareholders with more of a voice, only market-based solutions can give that voice impact through pitch and tone.

The Third Leg: Ethical and Moral Solutions

Wall Street failed to pick up on the public outrage over its skewed incentives and excessive pay. It was blind to how the industry looked from the outside. Consequently, new regulations were implemented. Market forces will enhance the effectiveness of regulatory intent. Both regulation and market forces can help to refurbish Wall Street's reputation—its "curb appeal."

Awakened by outside scrutiny and torrents of criticism, the financial industry has promised to change. But if the changes are merely cosmetic, superficial window dressing to placate regulators and shareholders, reform efforts will ultimately fail. A deeper ethical and moral reply is also required. Ultimately, character flows from neither the heavy hand of regulators nor the cool hand of markets.

The Bible teaches, "A good name is more desirable than great riches; to be esteemed is better than silver or gold" (Proverbs 22:1 NIV). The "good name" reference means not only external reputation but also foundational character. "Character is like a tree and reputation like a shadow. The shadow is what we think of it; the tree is the real thing," explained Abraham Lincoln.

Wall Street cast a dark shadow over the country during the credit crisis. But as we have also seen, finance can be "a shelter and shade from the heat of the day."[xciii] Each financial professional is, therefore, a guardian of the industry's reputation in addition to his or her own.

The credit crisis of 2008 swiftly threatened the entire financial system—demonstrating that Wall Street is indeed connected by the same root system. A healthy root system relies on culture-shaping influences. The Psalmist proclaims, "You cleared the ground for it, and it took root and filled the land."[xciv]

Neither regulation nor shareholder activism can reach into the root system of Wall Street. Companies can have extensive policies and procedures, but what do they actually practice? The *actual* choices and decisions practiced can be called "behavioral governance."[xcv]

Behavioral governance is really about people, rather than processes or policies. Codes of ethics are narrow, compliance-oriented documents. However, boards of directors must also monitor the company's culture and moral code. Wall Street firms routinely claim that its people are the firm's greatest assets—yet boards of directors repeatedly fail to recognize cultural drift within their organizations.

Because of Dodd-Frank's emphasis on shareholder rights, boards may be more reluctant to adjust numerical targets in a way that would reward executives for subpar performance. However, is there also an emphasis on the ethical treatment of employees, customers and suppliers? In this regard, faith traditions remind each of us of God's emphasis on the way we treat others.

Harvard professors Mahzarin R. Banaji, Max H. Bazerman, and Dolly Chugh approach the same subject through a wholly secular decision-making framework, yet arrive at the same conclusion: "Now pretend as you make your decisions, you don't know which group you belong to. . . . Would you be willing to risk being in the group disadvantaged by your decision? How would your decisions differ if you could make them wearing various identities not your own?"[xcvi]

Behavioral governance requires constantly examining the impact on others. For example, a familiar criticism of Wall Street is its overemphasis on short-term performance. A more subtle flaw, though, is the tendency to penalize patience.

All of the world's financial markets experience a never-ending cyclical series of ebbs and flows. It has often been wisely said about investing, "Sometimes doing nothing is doing something." [xcvii]

In this regard, markets are a lot like farming. One must work very hard to prepare the field for rain. However, incentive structures can't penalize waiting for the actual rain! This is what separates a relentless sales culture from one that tries to serve the interests of its clients.

In addition, helping customers manage risk does not always mean designing or selling something new. "I kind of believe that the best way to reduce risk is to take things out of the portfolio, not add them," said Ken Grant, president and founder of Risk Resources.[xcviii] An ethical culture elevates service to others over short-term profits. Incentive structures, therefore, need to reward stewardship that is measured by things like client retention, risk management, and safeguarding the firm's reputation. Incentives must also reflect the bigger picture, recognizing Wall Street's responsibility to serve the broader economy by putting capital to good use.

This requires harkening back to the very purpose and value of capital itself, outlined in Chapter 1. When invested in a productive business, capital blesses one's fellow man by increasing the productivity of labor and bringing prices down for consumers while raising wages for workers.

Recently, though, capital has become so abundant as a result of easy monetary policy that financiers "invested" paper wealth for the sole purpose of generating more paper wealth, none of which contributed to the production of real wealth that uplifts people. We are reminded, " . . . behold, all was vanity and vexation of spirit, and there was no profit under the sun."[xcix]

Capital needs to be valued and respected as a tool for lessening poverty, uplifting standards of living, and creating goods and services that enriches one's fellow man. But if capital becomes a plaything to be packaged into exotic instruments of dubious security, and then sold to unsuspecting investors to generate commissions and fees—an elaborate scheme to create "a lot of paper wealth"—then something good and worthy has been corrupted into something ignoble and pernicious.

SEC Commissioner Luis A. Aguilar articulated this notion: "And, we need to remember that capital formation is much more than just capital raising. True capital formation requires that funds raised be invested in productive assets."[c]

Although it isn't written into explicit mission statements, Wall Street is tasked with growing America's pie. That mission is best carried in the heart. A rising tide will lift all boats—including Wall Street's own. Such an attitude demands both selflessness and humility. As the Breton Fisherman's Prayer, given to him by Admiral Rickover, so poignantly reminded President John F. Kennedy, "O God the sea is so great and my boat is so small."

Whether it wants to admit it or not, Wall Street is part of a bigger ocean, and this reality should be reflected in compensation and incentives. Investment banks, for example, have long employed a metric known as the "compensation ratio," gauging pay as a percentage of firm revenues. Prior to the credit crisis, roughly 50 percent of company revenue was distributed to employees, including executives. This was standard industry practice.

However, the financial world must acknowledge that it is not immune to cyclical forces. In this regard, it is just like every other industry. Overall Wall Street profits were cut in *half* in 2011 ($13.5 billion versus $27.6 billion in 2010 and $61.4 billion in 2009).[ci] The declining profits picture undermines the appropriateness of the compensation ratio. Its continued use tramples shareholder rights.

Some experts say that over six years, investment banks spent three times as much on their staff as they generated in pretax profits for their shareholders.[cii] "In the tug of war between employees and shareholders, the employees are winning,"[ciii] banking analyst Mike Mayo told *The New York Times' Dealbook.* "Is the incentive pay an incentive, or is it an entitlement?"[civ]

After a near-death experience, Wall Street is being reshaped by regulatory forces that will restrain earnings for years to come. The industry needs to realize that it is not entitled to a larger share of a smaller pie simply because they became accustomed to a certain level of historical compensation. Future fat checks can't come in the form of shareholder subsidies, and therefore the practice of paying Wall Street bonuses out of purely paper trading profits or top-line revenue has to stop.

How much respect is shown for shareholders, employees and clients reflects a firm's moral and ethical culture. So does respect for the productive role of capital in society. Reaching for a smaller share of a larger pie is, in fact, the path to both greater and more sustainable prosperity. But this can only be accomplished by directly engaging broader society.

For example, Wall Street could build up a reservoir of good will by demonstrating a willingness to compromise—to say to the rest of America, "Meet me in the middle." In the area of compensation, the issue of the tax treatment of carried interest is a unique opportunity for Wall Street to show reasonableness. Private equity and hedge fund executives only pay the capital gains rate of 15 percent on most of their income instead of the ordinary income rate.

These firms charge their primarily institutional investors management fees (typically 1-2 percent annually) to cover the cost of operations of the fund. When management fees are taken as income, the manager is taxed at ordinary income rates (35 percent). Private equity and hedge funds also receive a success or performance fee for their services, usually keeping 20 percent of the profits earned on their investors' money. This additional fee earned is called "carried interest" and is taxed at the lower capital gains rate (15 percent).

Fortune Magazine's Dan Primack and others have made the reasoned case that carried interest really is a hybrid, and probably should be taxed somewhere in the middle. It's not the fund's own capital at risk, so they should not receive the same tax treatment as their investors. Yet, it is more than just a management fee—i.e., carried interest is only earned in the event of success.

While the industry heavily lobbied Congress to obtain the favorable tax treatment, a future willingness to compromise on carried interest would send a powerful signal. Too much groupthink has often prevented Wall Street from a balanced approach on many compensation-related issues.

There is also the issue of peer benchmarking. Compensation benchmarking is common for all job functions in all industries. Peer comparisons are an important part of how most people determine if they are being paid fairly. To show you how important it is, roughly half of rank-and-file respondents to a *Wall Street Journal FINS* informal survey said that they would turn down a dream job if their compensation would be 25 percent below the industry average.[cv]

It's not surprising that when CEOs compare themselves to others for salary negotiation purposes, they aim high. This type of attitude has inflated CEO salaries, with the pay practices of the average firm in an industry typically mimicking the industry leader.[cvi]

Every board of directors wants to tell shareholders that they have made an excellent CEO hire and therefore place their CEO in the top quartile of peer group pay. As part of the process, compensation consultants often "cherry-pick" peers, selecting slightly larger companies or those with more diversification of management responsibilities. The effect is to perpetually inflate pay for the entire sector.

Many people don't realize how challenging and all-encompassing it is to be a top executive in a large public company today. But, many CEOs must ask themselves, does keeping an average of 10 percent of their companies' net profits[cvii] promote win-win relationships? "CEOs deserve good pay but there's good pay and there's obscene pay," said Brian Wenzinger of Philadelphia money manager Aronson Johnson Ortiz.[cviii]

Much of this pay inflation stems from the fact that many CEOs measure their self-worth against their peers, demanding the same deal (or better) as other executives in the industry. As a result, money becomes the self-worth scoreboard.

Yet one of the lessons the financial crisis taught the world was that affluence can be fleeting, " . . . for riches certainly make themselves wings."[cix] For example, the share of total income garnered by America's top 1 percent of earners fell to 17.6 percent in 2009 after reaching an all-time high of 23.5 percent in 2007.[cx]

Great wealth is not a sign of virtue and God's favor, nor is it necessarily exploitative.[cxi] "While of course you can accumulate wealth through vice, it is possible to earn wealth through virtue and hold it in virtue—that is, discipline, vision, delayed gratification,"[cxii] writes Pastor Tim Keller of New York's Redeemer Presbyterian Church, whose congregation includes many financial professionals.

Jesus tells the wealthy young man who claimed to have followed all the commandments the one thing that he lacked: "Go sell everything you have and give to the poor, and you will have treasure in heaven. Then come, follow me."[cxiii] When the young man "went away sad," Keller explains that money had become the center of his identity.[cxiv] To give it away would have been to lose himself.[cxv]

Conscience unlocks doors that regulation and market forces simply can't reach. It reminds us that business is not a separate sphere. Giving to charity, for example, can't paper over reckless or selfish professional conduct.

In the same vein, the destructive forces of envy can't be permitted to overrun the just rewards of proper work. Madison warned against such "improper or wicked" schemes in *Federalist 10*. The Bible clearly states, "A heart at peace gives life to the body, but envy rots the bones."[cxvi]

Despite all the discussion of envy, that's not what is really at the heart of the income debate within the country. Many people are hurting from the Great Recession, hanging on by a very thin financial margin. What if the car breaks down? Who is going to watch the kids? Financial stress takes a steep psychological toll. Fear, lack of opportunity and discouragement, more than envy, are driving today's anti-capitalist sentiment.

At the Robin Hood Foundation's annual 2011 Heroes Breakfast, hedge fund titan Paul Tudor Jones gave a moving speech in which he referred to giving as "our defining grace" and expressed concern over an increasingly divided nation. Jones said, "Some liberals accuse the rich of being corrupt and greedy. Some conservatives accuse the poor of being lazy and entitled. I know both the rich and the poor pretty well, and I can tell you: Both of those statements are simply untrue, and they are grounded in ignorance."[cxvii]

The global financial crisis of 2008 showed us how fragilely connected we are. This interconnectedness means Wall Street's decisions have a profound impact on others. "Management is doing things right," said management guru Peter Drucker. "Leadership is doing the right things." Those "right things" can never fully be captured by a statute or reflected in a price.

Notes, Chapter 5

i The Collected Works of Abraham Lincoln edited by Roy P. Basler, Volume VII, "Reply to New York Workingmen's Democratic Republican Association" (March 21, 1864), pp. 259-260.

ii Bruce Bartlett, "Who Counts as 'Rich'? Continued," *The New York Times Economix*, December 13, 2011. http://economix.blogs.nytimes.com/2011/12/13/who-counts-as-rich-continued/.

iii Ibid.

iv Derek Kravitz, "4 million foreclosures subject to review," *Associated Press*, November 1, 2011. http://www.msnbc.msn.com/id/45122481/ns/business-real_estate/t/million-foreclosures-subject-review/.

v Julia Werdigier, "In Britain, Rising Outcry Over Executive Pay That Makes 'People's Blood Boil,'" *The New York Times*, January 22, 2012. http://www.nytimes.com/2012/01/23/business/in-britain-a-rising-outcry-over-lavish-executive-pay.html.

vi Nicholas Kristoff, "Is Banking Bad?," *The New York Times*, January 18, 2012. http://www.nytimes.com/2012/01/19/opinion/kristof-is-banking-bad.html.

vii Andrew Ross Sorkin, "Rich and Sort of Rich," *The New York Times*, May 14, 2011. http://www.nytimes.com/2011/05/15/weekinreview/15tax250copy.html.

viii "US Financial Services Industry: Contributing to a More Competitive US Economy," *Securities Industry and Financial Markets Association*, July 2010. http://www.ita.doc.gov/td/finance/publications/US percent20Financial percent20Services percent20Industry.pdf.

ix Benjamin Friedman, "Overmighty finance levies a tithe on growth," *The Financial Times*, August 26, 2009. http://www.ft.com/intl/cms/s/0/2de2b29a-9271-11de-b63b-00144feabdc0.html#axzz1vtv3AZoQ.

x Ibid.

xi "Who Exactly Are the 1 percent?," *The Economist*, January 21, 2012. http://www.economist.com/node/21543178.

xii Ibid.

xiii Robert G. Wilmers, "Small Banks, Big Banks: Giant Differences,"
Bloomberg, January 12, 2011.
http://www.bloomberg.com/news/2011-06-13/small-banks-big-banks-giant-differences-robert-g-wilmers.html.

xiv Nelson D. Schwartz, "Public Exit From Goldman Raises Doubt
Over a New Ethic," *The New York Times*, March 14, 2012.
http://www.nytimes.com/2012/03/15/business/a-public-exit-from-goldman-sachs-hits-a-wounded-wall-street.html?pagewanted=all.

xv Wilmers, "Small Banks, Big Banks: Giant Differences," January 12,
2011.

xvi Ibid.

xvii Sarah Stodola, "CEO Pay Survey: Big Payouts in Spite of
Recession," *The Fiscal Times*, April 21, 2011.
http://www.thefiscaltimes.com/Articles/2011/04/21/CEO-Pay-Survey-Big-Payouts-in-Spite-of-Recession.aspx#page1.

xviii John Weinbach, "Wall Street's $1 Million Fantasy League," *The
Wall Street Journal*, October 17, 2008.
http://online.wsj.com/article/SB122419823564442665.html.

xix "US Financial Services Industry: Contributing to a More
Competitive US Economy," *Securities Industry and Financial
Markets Association*, July 2010.

xx Peggy Noonan, "The Divider vs. the Thinker," *The Wall Street
Journal*, October 29, 2011.
http://online.wsj.com/article/SB1000142405297020355410457700
2262150454258.html.

xxi Andrew Ross Sorkin, "A Paradox of Smaller Wall Street
Paychecks," *The New York Times DealBook*, January 9, 2012.
http://dealbook.nytimes.com/2012/01/09/a-paradox-of-smaller-wall-street-paychecks/.

xxii Ibid.

xxiii Wilmers, "Small Banks, Big Banks: Giant Differences," January
12, 2011.

xxiv William Alden, "Study Says Wall Street Pay is Tilted Toward
White Men," *The New York Times DealBook*, December 2, 2011.
http://dealbook.nytimes.com/2011/12/02/study-sees-wall-street-pay-tilted-toward-white-men/.

xxv Jeff Cox, "Bank Layoffs Far From Over: 150,000 Likely in 2012: Bove," *CNBC*, December 16, 2011. http://www.cnbc.com/id/45696542/Bank_Layoffs_Far_From_Ove r_150_000_Likely_in_2012_Bove.

xxvi Dan Fitzpatrick and Rob Barry, "Ax Falls at Smaller Banks," *The Wall Street Journal*, November 30, 2011. http://online.wsj.com/article/SB1000142405297020376480457700 60752595022804.html.

xxvii James Madison, *The Federalist No. 51.*

xxviii Mervyn King speech to Scottish Business Organisations, Edinburgh, Scotland, October 20, 2009. http://www.bankofengland.co.uk/publications/Documents/speech es/2009/speech406.pdf.

xxix The Drucker Institute, Comment Letter to the SEC on Section 953(b) of Dodd-Frank, February 17, 2011. http://www.sec.gov/comments/df-title-ix/executive-compensation/executivecompensation-60.pdf.

xxx AFL-CIO Office of Investment, "How The SEC Can Minimize Dodd-Frank Section 953(b) Compliance Costs By Permitting the Use of Statistical Sampling to Calculate the Median."

xxxi Center on Executive Compensation, "Center on Executive Compensation Comments on the Use of Statistical Sampling to Implement Section 953(b) of the Dodd-Frank Wall Street Reform and Consumer Protection Act." http://www.sec.gov/comments/df-title-ix/executive-compensation/executivecompensation-79.pdf.

xxxii AFL-CIO Office of Investment, "Dodd-Frank Section 953(b): Why CEO-to-Worker Pay Ratios Matter for Investors."

xxxiii Ibid.

xxxiv Ibid.

xxxv Ilona Babenko, Benjamin Bennett, John M. Bizjak and Jeffrey L. Coles, "Clawback Provisions," March 15, 2012. http://papers.ssrn.com/sol3/papers.cfm?abstract_id=2023292.

xxxvi Ibid.

xxxvii Ibid.

xxxviii Carla Main, "Pay Clawback, Basel Bank Failure, OSC Probe, Bank Stress Test: Compliance," *Bloomberg*, July 7, 2011.

http://www.bloomberg.com/news/2011-07-07/pay-clawback-basel-bank-failure-osc-probe-compliance.html.

xxxix Liz Moyer, "On 'Bleak' Street, Bosses in Cross Hairs," *The Wall Street Journal*, February 8, 2012. http://online.wsj.com/article/SB1000142405297020413640457720 9383447837986.html.

xl Gonzalo Vina, "Barclays CEO Pay 'Corrosive' for U.K. Economy, Study Says," Bloomberg, November 22, 2011. http://www.bloomberg.com/news/2011-11-22/barclays-diamond-s-pay-corrosive-for-u-k-economy-study-says.html.

xli Susanne Craig, "Modest Year on Wall St., but Stock Could Yield Fortunes," *The New York Times Dealbook*, December 3, 2011. http://dealbook.nytimes.com/2011/12/03/modest-bonus-year-on-wall-st-but-stock-could-yield-fortunes/.

xlii David Kocieniewski, "Tax Benefits from Options as Windfall for Businesses," *The New York Times*, December 29, 2011. http://www.nytimes.com/2011/12/30/business/tax-breaks-from-options-a-windfall-for-businesses.html?pagewanted=all.

xliii John Mauldin, "The Transparency Trap," *Front Line Thoughts*, January 30, 2012. http://www.johnmauldin.com/frontlinethoughts/the-transparency-trap.

xliv Ibid.

xlv Ibid.

xlvi Roger Martin, "Bank CEOs and the infinite pile of cash," *Reuters*, October 5th, 2011. http://blogs.reuters.com/great-debate/2011/10/05/bank-ceos-and-the-infinite-pile-of-cash/.

xlvii Ibid.

xlviii Ibid.

xlix Paul A. Volcker, "Commentary on the Restrictions on Proprietary Trading by Insured Depositary Institutions." http://online.wsj.com/public/resources/documents/Volcker_Rule_Essay_2-13-12.pdf.

l Devin Leonard, "Dick Parsons, Captain Emergency," *Bloomberg Businessweek*, March 24, 2011. http://www.businessweek.com/magazine/content/11_14/b4222084044889.htm.

li Mayo, *Exile on Wall Street: One Analyst's Fight to Save the Big Banks From Themselves*, Kindle 129.

lii David Enrich, "J.P. Morgan Holding Talks with U.K. Regulators," *The Wall Street Journal*, May 11, 2012. http://online.wsj.com/article/SB100014240527023042036045773 97592721419140.html.

liii Nelson D. Schwartz, "A Shock from JP Morgan Is New Fodder for Reformers," *The New York Times DealBook*, May 10, 2012. http://dealbook.nytimes.com/2012/05/10/a-shock-from-jpmorgan-is-new-fodder-for-reformers/.

liv Zachary Karabell, "JP Morgan's 2 Billion Loss Fueled by Efforts to Avoid Risk," *The Daily Beast*, May 11, 2012. http://www.thedailybeast.com/articles/2012/05/11/jp-morgan-s-2-billion-loss-fueled-by-efforts-to-avoid-risk.html.

lv Ibid.

lvi Aaron Task, "Jamie Dimon Hearing, Explained: 'Frustrating, Maddening, Comical,'" *Yahoo Finance*, June 13, 2012. http://finance.yahoo.com/blogs/daily-ticker/jamie-dimon-hearing-explained-frustrating-maddening-comical-181114289.html.

lvii Joe Nocera, "*When Will They Learn?*," *The New York Times*, May 11, 2012. http://www.nytimes.com/2012/05/12/opinion/nocera-when-will-they-learn.html.

lviii Peter Eavis, "JPMorgan's Deficient Disclosures," *The New York Times Dealbook*, May 24, 2012, http://dealbook.nytimes.com/2012/05/24/jpmorgans-deficient-disclosures/?nl=business&emc=edit_dlbkpm_20120524.

lix James Pethokoukis, "Financial Reform and the hubris of Timothy Geithner," *The American*, March 2, 2012. http://blog.american.com/2012/03/financial-reform-and-the-hubris-of-timothy-geithner/.

lx Andrew Frye and Natalie Doss, "Buffet Compares Wall Street to Church with Raffle," *Bloomberg*, October 5, 2010. http://www.bloomberg.com/news/2010-10-05/buffett-compares-wall-street-casino-culture-to-church-raffles.html.

lxi Nassim Nicholas Taleb, "End Bonuses for Bankers," *The New York Times*, November 7, 2011.

http://www.nytimes.com/2011/11/08/opinion/end-bonuses-for-bankers.html.

lxii Ibid.

lxiii Ibid.

lxiv Michael Schuman, "How to Save Capitalism," *Time*, January 19, 2012. http://business.time.com/2012/01/19/how-to-save-capitalism/.

lxv Becket Adams, "Lawmakers Anxious to Enact Dodd-Frank Reg Forcing Disclosure of CEO Pay," *The Blaze*, March 9, 2012. http://www.theblaze.com/stories/lawmakers-anxious-to-enact-dodd-frank-reg-forcing-disclosure-of-ceo-pay/.

lxvi Ibid.

lxvii Julia Werdigier, "In Britain, Rising Outcry Over Executive Pay That Makes 'People's Blood Boil,'" *The New York Times*, January 22, 2012. http://www.nytimes.com/2012/01/23/business/in-britain-a-rising-outcry-over-lavish-executive-pay.html.

lxviii Ibid.

lxix Svenja O'Donnell, "Cameron Pledges Vote for Shareholders on 'Wrong' Executive Pay Rewards," *Bloomberg*, January 8, 2012. http://www.bloomberg.com/news/2012-01-08/cameron-pledges-vote-for-shareholders-on-wrong-executive-pay.html.

lxx Marc S. Gerber, "US corporate governance challenges: Say-on-pay, proxy access, Dodd-Frank and potentially more auditor independence rules," *Thomson Reuters*, March 20, 2012. http://newsandinsight.thomsonreuters.com/Legal/Insight/2012/03_-_March/U_S__corporate_governance_challenges__Say-on-pay,_proxy_access,_Dodd-Frank_and_potentially_more_auditor_independence_rules/.

lxxi Ibid.

lxxii Eleanor Bloxham, "HP: Same issues, different year," *Fortune*, February 10, 2012. http://management.fortune.cnn.com/2012/02/10/hp-same-issues-different-year/.

lxxiii Carl T. Hagberg, "What to do about the annual meeting?," *Directors and Boards*, Vol. 35, No.2, First Quarter 2011. http://www.shareholderforum.com/emtg/Library/2011Q1_Directors percent20& percent20Boards-articles.pdf.

lxxiv Ibid.

lxxv Catherine Dunn, "Lagging Wall Street Bonuses Through the Lens of Public Opinion," *Corporate Counsel*, November 9, 2011. http://www.law.com/jsp/cc/PubArticleCC.jsp?id=1202529850054
.

lxxvi "Ownership of Mutual Funds, Shareholder Sentiment, and Use of the Internet, 2010," *Investment Company Institute*, September 2010. http://www.ici.org/pdf/fm-v19n6.pdf.

lxxvii Deborah Brewster, "Retail investors in US equities hits low," *The Financial Times*, September 1, 2008. http://www.ft.com/intl/cms/s/0/c92d888a-7871-11dd-acc3-0000779fd18c.html#axzz1vtv3AZoQ.

lxxviii Ibid.

lxxix Julia Werdigier, "In Britain, Rising Outcry Over Executive Pay That Makes 'People's Blood Boil,'" January 22, 2012.

lxxx Charles M. Nathan, "The Future of Institutional Share Voting: Three Paradigms," *The Harvard Law School Forum on Corporate Governance and Financial Regulation*, July 23, 2010. http://blogs.law.harvard.edu/corpgov/2010/07/23/the-future-of-institutional-share-voting-three-paradigms/.

lxxxi Ibid.

lxxxii Charles M. Nathan, "The Future of Institutional Share Voting Revisited: A Fourth Paradigm," *The Harvard Law School Forum on Corporate Governance and Financial Regulation*, September 27, 2011.

lxxxiii Ibid.

lxxxiv Hagberg, "What to do about the annual meeting?," First Quarter 2011

lxxxv Ibid.

lxxxvi Kaja Whitehouse, "Advisory firm employee leaking shareholder voting data, whistleblower claims," *The New York Post*, April 10, 2012. http://www.nypost.com/p/news/business/fraud_by_proxy_tT8Sea WrBBCVkJePZRTQQM.

lxxxvii Nathan, "The Future of Institutional Share Voting Revisited: A Fourth Paradigm," September 27, 2011.

lxxxviii Joann S. Lublin, "Executive Pay Votes Spur Shifts in Policies," *The Wall Street Journal*, March 1, 2012. http://online.wsj.com/article/SB1000142405297020457140457725564 1531516510.html?mod=djkeyword#printMode.

lxxxix David Hunkar, "Duration of Stock Holding Periods Continue to Fall Globally," *TopForeignStocks.com*, September 6, 2010. http://topforeignstocks.com/2010/09/06/duration-of-stock-holding-period-continues-to-fall-globally/.

xc Dr. Carr Bettis interview with the author, December 20, 2011.

xci Werdigier, "In Britain, Rising Outcry Over Executive Pay That Makes 'People's Blood Boil,'" January 22, 2012.

xcii Ibid.

xciii The Holy Bible: Isaiah 4:6 (NIV).

xciv The Holy Bible: Psalm 80:9 (NIV).

xcv Bettis interview with the author.

xcvi Mahzarin R. Banaji, Max H. Bazerman, and Dolly Chugh, "How (Un)ethical Are You?," *Harvard Business Review*, December 2003. http://hbr.org/2003/12/how-unethical-are-you/ar/1.

xcvii

xcviii Azam Ahmed, "New Investment Strategy: Preparing for End Times," *The New York Times DealBook*, June 29, 2011. http://dealbook.nytimes.com/2011/06/29/a-new-investment-strategy-preparing-for-end-times/.

xcix The Holy Bible: Ecclesiastes 2:11 (KJV).

c Remarks by SEC Commissioner Luis A. Aguilar SEC Government Business Forum on Small Business Capital Formation, November 17, 2011. https://www.secondmarket.com/discover/wp-content/uploads/2012/01/2011-Final-Report-SEC-Govt-Business-Forum-on-Small-Business-Capital-Formation.pdf.

ci Ibid.

cii WilliamWright, "Dividing the spoils between bankers and shareholders," *Financial News*, February 21, 2012. http://www.efinancialnews.com/story/2012-02-21/dividing-the-spoils-between-bankers-and-shareholders.

ciii Andrew Ross Sorkin, "A Paradox of Smaller Wall Street Paychecks," *The New York Times Dealbook*, January 9, 2012.

civ Ibid.

cv Kelly Eggers, "Why It's Okay to Get Paid Less," *FINS Technology*, January 15, 2011. http://it-jobs.fins.com/Articles/SB130816636352923783/Why-It-s-Okay-to-Get-Paid-Less.

cvi Ivan E. Bruck, Darius Palia, and Chia-Jane Wang, "Industry Effects and Relative Pay for Relative Performance", March 7, 2012. http://www90.homepage.villanova.edu/michael.pagano/IB percent20bpw_03_15_2012.pdf.

cvii Lucian Bebchuk and Yaniv Grinstein, "The Growth of Executive Pay", *Oxford Review of Economic Policy*, Vol 21 (2005). http://papers.ssrn.com/sol3/papers.cfm?abstract_id=648682.

cviii Jessica Silver-Greenberg and Nelson D. Schwartz, "Citigroup's Chief Rebuffed on Pay by Shareholders," *The New York Times DealBook*, April 17, 2012. http://dealbook.nytimes.com/2012/04/17/citigroup-shareholders-reject-executive-pay-plan/.

cix The Holy Bible: Proverbs 23:5 (KJV).

cx *The Economist*, "Who Exactly Are the 1 percent?," January 21, 2012.

cxi Tim Keller, *King's Cross: The Story of the World in the Life of Jesus* (New York: Dutton Adult, 2011), 125.

cxii Ibid.

cxiii The Holy Bible: Mark 10: 18-22 (ESV).

cxiv Keller, *King's Cross: The Story of the World in the Life of Jesus*, 129.

cxv Ibid.

cxvi The Holy Bible: Proverbs 14:30 (NIV).

cxvii Paul Tudor Jones speech to the 22nd Annual Heroes Awards Breakfast. http://www.valuewalk.com/2011/12/2011-heroes-breakfast-closing-remarks-paul-tudor-jones-ii/.

6   A Bad Neighborhood

Honesty is such a lonely word
Everyone is so untrue
Honesty is hardly ever heard
And mostly what I need from you
      – Billy Joel, "Honesty" (1979)

Effective regulation, market discipline, and higher ethical and moral standards are the formula for a healthier, more stable and more respected Wall Street. One piece is still missing, though, and that is trust. Up to this point, advocates for each of these three solutions have operated almost exclusively in separate spheres. Only trust can weave the solutions together and connect them to the public. Trust is often elusive in interpersonal relationships, however, as it requires moving beyond blame, a shared acceptance of responsibility, and frank honesty.

Wall Street's dishonesty nearly toppled the financial system. Information asymmetries abounded. Bank balance sheets reeked of concealment. The marketing materials and ratings of securitized mortgage derivatives failed to adequately disclose serious conflicts of interest. The risks of teaser rates and interest-only mortgages were often not made clear to unsophisticated borrowers.

This pervasive lack of truthfulness and honesty built up quickly. "The period from 2000 to 2008 saw a very large accumulation of hidden exposures in the financial system," wrote author Nassim Taleb.[i]

Some understood the problems and looked the other way. Others refused to heed the warnings. Many simply stopped searching for the truth or incorrectly assumed that someone surely must be on guard to protect investors from danger.

The truth, however, was ultimately revealed in time: "For whatever is hidden is meant to be disclosed, and whatever is concealed is meant to be brought out into the open."[ii]

Eventually, it became clear that client interests were not being honored within segments of the financial industry. Risk was transferred to those least likely to understand it, including less sophisticated professional investors both domestic and foreign, violating a duty of trust to all. The goal for many on Wall Street was to sell whatever would produce the largest commissions, regardless of whether the investments suited the client's objectives. Derivatives trading was the ultimate zero-sum game with essentially no value creation. "You have to realize this is a game of musical chairs. When the music stops, the person or bank that has the assets sitting on his books loses,"[iii] said Rasanath Das, a former investment banker who specialized in structured products and mortgage-backed securities before becoming a Hindu monk.

The reality is, though, that greed also darkened many hearts far beyond Wall Street. Derivative bets didn't affect whether homeowners defaulted. As the facts fully emerged about the financial meltdown, it became abundantly clear that this was an *American* crisis of truth.

Each Speaking the Truth

"And you shall know the truth, and the truth shall make you free."
— John 8:32

There is a fundamental relationship between truth and trust. Trust is an honor—a reward that must be earned. The Bible says, "Therefore, having put away falsehood, let each one of you speak the truth with his neighbor, for we are members one of another."[iv] A community can't develop unless each speaks the truth to his neighbor.

In this regard, the search for truth and trust can't stop exclusively at Wall Street's doorstep. Nursing an offense against a wrongdoer can often blind us to our own faults. The "plank in our own eye"[v] prevents us from judging ourselves by the same standard we apply to our neighbor. Many judge others by their actions but judge themselves by their intentions.[vi]

Any meaningful moral accounting requires Washington and the American people each to own up to their respective responsibilities in the financial crisis and also commit to a new code of ethics. As Mark Twain wittily noted, "Nothing so needs reforming as other people's habits."

Hold up a mirror to the financial industry, and a country in denial should also see itself. That is because the origins of the financial crisis can be found in the massive run-up in home prices primarily during the years 2004 to 2006. During that time, a disturbing number of homebuyers engaged in flagrant fraud or misrepresentation on their mortgage applications. Others knowingly "gamed" a system in which commission-based mortgage brokers routinely failed to verify standard information about their borrowers, such as income or credit history. In some cases, mortgage brokers did not even ask for the information.

Real estate speculators, mostly ordinary Americans, greatly exacerbated the crisis, particularly in states like Arizona, California, Florida and Nevada. Many began viewing housing as strictly a financial asset for resale. Fueled by infomercials and seminars, house "flipping" was an alluring get-rich-quick scheme that required little experience and was made possible by large amounts of cheap financing. These speculators relied heavily on leverage to buy multiple properties. Inevitably, the bubble burst, and they defaulted at alarming rates.

In September 2004, the FBI began publicly warning that there was a "growing epidemic" of mortgage fraud in the country.[vii] This included rampant "occupancy fraud," cases where an investor falsely claimed on the mortgage application that he intended to occupy the property as a primary residence.[viii] In so doing, the speculator could obtain a lower rate of interest and a smaller down payment. That is because it was a well-established fact in the mortgage-lending industry that owner-occupants were far less likely to walk away from a distressed property than investors.

Some studies found that over 90 percent of all subprime borrowers in 2004-2006 claimed to be owner-occupants.[ix] Others estimated that 10 percent of all mortgage applications during the period involved fraud and that 25 percent of all foreclosures involved some kind of application misrepresentation.[x] Just as the FBI had predicted, a cancerous lack of truthfulness on the part of ordinary Americans played an important role in contributing to the housing collapse.

How caught up was the American public in the housing mania? Researchers at the Federal Reserve Bank of New York found that at the peak of the boom in 2006, over a third of all US home purchase lending was made to people who already owned at least one house.[xi] In the four states with the biggest housing bubbles (Arizona, California, Florida and Nevada), the investor share was 45 percent,[xii] doubling between 2000 and 2006.[xiii] In 2006, investors in these states owning three or more properties were responsible for nearly 20 percent of originations, almost triple their share in 2000.[xiv]

Speculators were only part of the problem, though. A sense of entitlement could be found in almost every neighborhood in America. A growing number of Americans refused to own up to their own irresponsible actions. Most people knew someone who simply elected to stop paying their mortgage because their house's value had depreciated so dramatically. A cottage industry of lawyers developed to encourage "underwater" homeowners (typically with little or no home equity) to violate the sanctity of contract and rights of creditors, even when those individuals had the means to keep paying on the mortgage. Those that engaged in such "strategic defaults" were often able to live in the house mortgage-free for months or years before the commencement of any adverse action from their lending institution. At the same time, neighbors who played by the rules and were struggling to stay current on their own mortgages in a bad economy looked on with growing frustration. Ironically, it was those solvent, never-miss-a-mortgage-payment Americans who were expected to pay to bail out the banks.

The higher the price of the home, the more reluctant banks were to foreclose. Banks are notoriously lousy marketers of real estate and therefore go to greater lengths to avoid commencing foreclosure actions on harder-to-sell luxury properties. Once the bank forecloses, the financial institution is also forced to pay the back taxes and often a five-figure maintenance bill to get the property into marketable condition. It should come as no surprise then that borrowers with loans of at least $1 million were in default for an average 792 days last year before banks repossessed their homes versus an average of 611 days for loans under $250,000—a difference of about six months.[xv]

"We are the only country in the world where you can borrow money on a house and walk away from it. Everywhere else, all the people in Europe, all the people who borrow money in Brazil, they're all personally liable for 100 percent of the debt,"[xvi] said influential real estate mogul Sam Zell. "So by virtue of not being personally liable, we've created a giant moral hazard."[xvii]

Others treated their primary residence like an ATM, borrowing against the value of their home to splurge on consumer goods. A 2011 report from real estate data firm CoreLogic, Inc. revealed that 38 percent of homeowners with second mortgages were underwater—that is, the borrower owed more than the value of their home.[xviii] Perhaps most telling was the fact that only 18 percent of homeowners who didn't take out a second mortgage were underwater.[xix]

None of these events could have happened, though, without the distorting hand of government. Fannie Mae and Freddie Mac, the Department of Housing and Urban Development, and the US Federal Reserve all had their fingerprints on the housing bubble.

Speaking of the government-sponsored credit bubble that overstimulated housing, former Treasury Secretary Henry Paulson said in 2012, "Financial crises stem from flawed government policies. Always."[xx] Paulson explained that these flawed policies were hardly peripheral to the crisis and exacerbated Americans' propensity to borrow too much and save too little.

"Because the banks always make mistakes, so people pile on the banks," Paulson continued, "and they work to correct those mistakes."[xxi] Applauding the fact that much had been done to strengthen the banking system since the crisis, he warned, "But the government policies that got us here, no one's dealt with those big issues, and those are the issues we really need to deal with."[xxii]

Extending Trust to Receive It

"The only way to make a man trustworthy is to trust him."
– Henry L. Stimson

Why haven't we dealt with the big issues? In part, it's because trust issues rest on mutuality, an elusive concept in our current society. Building trust often requires first extending it to others.

President Obama conceded that " . . . there is a deficit of trust between this town (Washington) and the rest of the country."[xxiii] However, time and again since the onset of the crisis, governments around the world acted as if they did not believe the public can handle the truth about the state of the financial system. Instead, financial emergency responses were often cloaked in secrecy and loaded with paternalism.

William K. Black, Associate Professor of Economics and Law at the University of Missouri–Kansas City, said that rather than let the public know how bad things really were, " . . . the entire strategy is to keep people from getting the facts."[xxiv] The American people, however, have a right to share in the full truth, no matter hard it may be—not a softer version of the truth that better fits someone's political narrative.

The truth underlying the financial crisis is not pretty. The story starts with former Fed Chairman Alan Greenspan's refusal to trust the signs of economic recovery in the years following the September 11 attacks. Instead, he kept interest rates too low for too long, thereby enabling the housing bubble that ensued.

In a prolonged low-interest-rate environment, supposedly sophisticated global investors, including hedge funds, insurance companies, pensions, and sovereign wealth funds reached for yield, often regardless of credit quality and without conducting proper due diligence. Some of these investors would later sue the banks, prompting J.P. Morgan CEO Jamie Dimon to tell shareholders in 2012 that he would oppose " . . . securities claims brought by sophisticated investors who understood and accepted the risks."[xxv] There was a nearly insatiable appetite for the highest yielding mortgage-backed securities, bundles of mortgages given to the least creditworthy ("subprime") borrowers.

Nonbank originators, thrifts and other trading platforms, operating outside of most regulations and enabled by watered-down Fannie Mae underwriting standards, sprang up to make subprime loans and facilitate the creation of these high-yield mortgage products. Yet, Mr. Greenspan and others failed to recognize the explosive emergence of this so-called "shadow" banking system.

All the large financial institutions soon joined the mortgage derivatives gold rush. In so doing, the biggest banks became heavily exposed to the same asset class and risks. They were aided by willing ratings agencies that were paid by the investment banks for advice on how to structure the same exotic instruments that they would later rate. To keep the fees coming and also satisfy their own public shareholders, ratings agencies had a strong incentive to assign the highest possible ratings to these risky securities. At the same time, the ratings agencies enjoyed blanket First Amendment protection for their ratings that were legally considered "opinions," but too often believed by investors to be fact.

Wall Street business models then gravitated toward these leverage-fueled, high-margin activities. Gone were the days of bread-and-butter banking that rested largely upon borrowing money in the form of customer deposits and lending it out at higher rates based upon knowledge of the local community. In its place rose a jumbled and dangerous concentrated hybrid of depository banking and speculative proprietary trading. Federal deposit insurance, which originated during the New Deal, reduced customer scrutiny that would have otherwise reigned in banker recklessness.[xxvi]

The same is true today. As of Dec. 31, 2010, the six largest US banks held 36 percent of domestic deposits compared to only 9 percent in 1990.[xxvii] At the same time, the six largest bank holding companies generated 74 percent of their pretax income in 2010 from trading revenue—which represented 93 percent of the trading revenue produced by all American banks.[xxviii] Citing these statistics, Robert G. Wilmers, the chairman and CEO of M&T Bank Corp. wrote, "To say these large institutions are the same species as traditional commercial banks is akin to describing dinosaurs as reptiles—true but profoundly misleading."[xxix]

More than any other activity, proprietary trading contained the largest concentration of embedded conflicts of interest. In other areas, like investment banking, for example, a firm's motivations and incentives were readily understood by clients. But when that firm traded the same instruments for its own profit (or loss) as well as simultaneously on behalf of clients, while often using the same personnel to do so, it opened a Pandora's box of ethical dilemmas around sales, marketing and disclosure practices. Former Fed Chairman Paul Volcker said proprietary trading took place "often at the expense of customer relationships."[xxx]

When things later unraveled, policymakers decided that financial firms and their highly leveraged proprietary trading activities had become so interconnected that the receivership mechanisms established by the George H.W. Bush administration during the savings and loan crisis to manage insolvent firms were now inadequate. The S&L industry had pushed the envelope in the 1980s, expanding beyond its traditional purpose of promoting home ownership into risky construction loans. Initially, regulators compounded the problem by allowing insolvent S&Ls to remain open and additional losses to accumulate.

The S&L debacle should have served both as a warning to Wall Street and a roadmap for emergency management of insolvent institutions. In response to the S&L crisis, new laws were quickly passed, such as the Prompt Corrective Action Law that required regulators to promptly shutter failed institutions. These laws were not fully adequate to address all the issues of the 2008 crisis. For example, while the FDIC acts as the receiver in cases involving insolvent banks, there was insufficient regulatory authority to oversee the orderly resolution of a systemically important nonbank financial firm. The general framework erected after the S&L debacle, however, should have served as a valuable starting point.

Washington did not trust the lessons of that framework, though. Instead, an experimental "economic green zone" was erected around large financial institutions. In order to accomplish this, the Federal Reserve and its chairman, Ben Bernanke, embarked on the most accommodative monetary policy in the nation's history, injecting $12.2 trillion[xxxi] of liquidity into the financial system through various lending and bailout facilities. This buffet of unconventional policy tools was aimed at propping up the prices of toxic assets. While effective, the approach did not allow for market-clearing price discovery.

With the banks stabilized, the Federal Reserve later followed with two rounds of so-called "quantitative easing" (QE) or debt monetization, purchasing over $2 trillion of mortgage and government securities to further drive down interest rates by bidding up Treasury prices and taking supply off the market. Quantitative easing gave money to the banks with the expectation they would lend it into the real economy. In practice, banks used QE to purchase stocks and other financial assets. With a banking system awash in reserves, other financial institutions were content to simply exploit the interest spread between the federal funds' overnight loan rate and Treasury yields. At the onset of the financial crisis, the Fed began paying banks interest on reserves – thereby reducing incentives to lend into the real economy. In a highly unusual move, the Fed encouraged additional buying of risk assets like stocks by openly assuring financial markets that it would keep short-term interest rates near zero until 2014.

Through all these various techniques, critics charged the Federal Reserve sought to ultimately address a deep-seated solvency and trust crisis with the very same leverage that fueled the crisis itself—but on a larger scale. The result so far has been a classic "liquidity trap" with diminishing returns from each subsequent wave of easing. The Fed has been quick to claim, however, that it generated $77.4 billion[xxxii] in profits for the taxpayers during 2011 from both rounds of asset purchases and the repayment of almost all the emergency loans it extended. Alas, those profits are no more substantial than the credit that was conjured up to produce them. However, the cost of these profits has included the leveraging up of the Fed's own balance sheet to nearly $3 trillion, a pace that would keep even the most aggressive hedge fund manager awake at night.

As a result, Texas congressman and presidential candidate Ron Paul referred to the Federal Reserve as "immoral."[xxxiii] Perhaps a more appropriate description would be "paternalistic." By seeking to micromanage the world's largest economy and perpetually soften outcomes long after the worst of the financial crisis had passed, the Fed appeared unwilling to trust the American people with finding a new, albeit bumpy, economic "normal." Nor would the Fed engage in an honest conversation with the American people about the tradeoffs between future inflation risks and artificially sustained consumption.

In contrast, former Fed Chairman Paul Volcker earned great respect by demonstrating his resolve to make the truly difficult choices needed to whip inflation in the early 1980s. This included making the case that bitter, but necessary, medicine would be required. While unpopular at first, markets grew to admire Volcker's resolve when a sustained economic expansion later took hold.

By not sorting out the economy's excesses, it raised the likelihood that the Bernanke Federal Reserve was laying the groundwork for the next speculative bubble. In so doing, the Federal Reserve and other global monetary authorities perpetuated two trust-killing conditions: a sense of timid dependence and self-indulgent entitlement.

Dependence

"Dependence begets subservience and venality, suffocates the germ of virtue, and prepares fit tools for the designs of ambition,"
– Thomas Jefferson

Many of the elements of the unfolding credit crisis were truly unprecedented and therefore demanded creative, emergency responses. Chairman Bernanke and his colleagues on the Federal Reserve Board were operating under extraordinarily difficult conditions during much of 2008. The speed and complexity of the problems demanded unconventional actions and broad latitude.

Fast forward to 2012: Despite a dramatic recovery in asset prices and gradual improvement in the real economy, the Federal Reserve has been unwilling to even prepare the ground for an eventual exit from its expanded role. Appearing intoxicated with the notion that it can pull all the right levers, the Fed continues to tinker with the economy. But the longer the Federal Reserve casts its hulking shadow over the economy, the more financial markets become dependent on continued state-sponsored liquidity and artificially low interest rates.

As if that weren't dangerous enough, independent monetary policy can, itself, be co-opted by the political class. The financial crisis and Great Recession were only one piece of a larger debt super-cycle that saw borrowing balloon at the household, corporate and government level. When the credit bubble burst, the government leapt into the vacuum created by households and corporations beginning the necessary de-leveraging process. As a result, both Wall Street and millions of Americans citizens have become more dependent on Washington than ever before. Dependency, however, is *not* trust. Trust must be perpetually earned, while dependency is opportunistically captured.

American, Japanese and European government leaders across the ideological spectrum have not leveled with their people about the state of fiscal imbalances and the techniques being used to cope with them. In the end, a debt crisis cannot be solved by more debt.

There is a specific term for measures that heavily indebted governments employ to channel money to themselves without having to submit to the legislative process: it's known as financial repression. First employed exclusively in the developing world and later in Japan, these measures allow governments to issue debt at lower interest rates than would otherwise be possible, thereby reducing debt service costs.

Most of the world's leading industrial economies are now simultaneously engaged in the same practice of manipulating interest rates to levels below the rate of price inflation. "A large role for non-market forces in interest-rate determination is a central feature of financial repression," writes esteemed financial crisis scholar Carmen Reinhart.[xxxiv]

By capping longer-dated sovereign debt at nominal interest rates below the rate of inflation (i.e., negative real interest rates), repression acts as a stealth tax on bondholders and savers by eroding the value of government debt. This more painless form of de-leveraging is attractive to governments because it doesn't require convincing the public to accept what in Europe is currently referred to as "austerity," a buzzword that means: cuts in government spending.

But in order for financial repression to work, government must pull the financial sector more fully into its orbit. This is easier to accomplish when the banking sector is highly concentrated in a handful of large institutions. As a component of this gravitational pull toward greater government control, financial repression can operate as a breeding ground for "regulatory capture," a condition where regulatory agencies become increasingly sympathetic and allied to the industry they oversee. Management may also be placed in the untenable position of serving two masters, shareholders and politicians, creating internal confusion and damaging moral.

Financial repression is not just a theoretical technique for academic discussion, though. Governments are increasingly relying on captive domestic banks to absorb the massive supply of sovereign debt issuance. Since governments must maintain unfettered access to the debt markets, they backstop too-big-to-fail primary dealers at all costs.

The European Central Bank (ECB), for example, postponed a looming financial crisis in late 2011 by lending over a trillion dollars of 1 percent money to Eurozone banks for three years against essentially any quality of collateral. While the Long-Term Refinancing Operation (LTRO) ignited a sharp global equity market rally in the first quarter of 2012, it did little to influence the demand for credit in Europe and also swelled the central bank's balance sheet to unprecedented levels. Central bank balance sheets around the world have doubled in just a decade, now containing $18 trillion of assets or roughly 30 percent of global gross domestic product.[xxxv]

Many of the financial institutions used the three-year re-funding program to hoist poor-quality bonds onto the European Central Bank's balance sheet as collateral, further ensuring the interconnectedness of Europe's institutions. With each passing day, Europe's taxpayers increasingly function as *both* guarantors and debtors.

Perhaps most importantly, the ECB's liquidity injection ensured a captive market for European sovereign debt as European banks, flush with cheap 1 percent money, snapped up higher-yielding short-term Italian, Spanish and Eurozone periphery government bonds, allowing the banks to turn an easy profit on the interest rate spread while also keeping a lid on spiking sovereign borrowing costs. Many saw this as an under-the-table way to bail out wobbling states by funneling cash to their domestic banking sector. The existing European Union Treaty and the European Central Bank's own founding charter prohibit the ECB from functioning as the lender of last resort to insolvent nations, yet that result was accomplished by the LTRO via the pass-through conduit of Europe's financial institutions.

The ultimate irony of enabling Europe's financial sector to engage in this type of so-called "carry trade" strategy was that banks were being encouraged to double down on the *same* troubled sovereign bonds that crippled their balance sheets in the first place. Since many believed it was inconceivable that any Eurozone country could default, regulators had previously allowed European banks to employ highly aggressive leverage (often 30 times) to load up on sovereign debt without having to maintain normal levels of reserves against potential losses. On the brink of collapse, regulators turned a blind eye again and allowed European banks to extend their balance sheets even further. Politicians such as former French President Nicolas Sarkozy applauded as banks used the latest LTRO funding and substantial leverage to once again support new government borrowing. There simply weren't enough buyers of government debt without European bank participation. At the same time, domestic banking regulators of several European nations were reluctant to allow banks to sell unprofitable operations for fear of the impact on their local economies.

With access to funding assured, European banks also largely resisted raising additional equity. The question becomes, what happens in three years when the ECB loans need to be refinanced? It likely creates a further dependency between the banking sector and the state, a hallmark of financial repression, as banks become addicted to easy financing rather than taking the necessary (although likely costly and dilutive) steps to improve their capital position. The ECB also ensured its own survival as a power-wielding institution by preserving European unification.

An increasingly tight connection between government and banks is by no means exclusive to Europe. America's own extraordinary financing needs also increasingly depend on demand from captive financial institutions. Given the desire to avoid a repeat of the 2008 financial crisis, banks are required to hold a higher amount of lower risk-weighted assets. US government debt functions as the asset of choice to meet these stricter requirements.

In addition, Treasury bonds serve as collateral among global banks nervously loaning money to each other. As derivatives transactions migrate to exchanges under Dodd-Frank, institutions will also have to post margin, often in the form of Treasuries. It should then come as no surprise that US banks bought more Treasuries and government agency securities in the first two months of 2012 ($78.2 billion) than they did in all of 2011.[xxxvi]

Both a Fence *and* a Mirror

"We took risks. We knew we took them. Things have come out against us. We have no cause for complaint."
    – *Robert Frost*

"For each will have to bear his own load."
    – *Galatians 6:5*

Just as trust cannot rest on dependency, nor can it rest on expectation – an entitled sense that others will subsidize one's bad choices. One of capitalism's long-standing and most effective traits is its ability to weed out and curtail inept or reckless behavior. Capital can be misallocated, thereby distorting markets and misdirecting production into wasteful and uneconomic channels. Corrections, while painful, cleanse malinvestment and set the stage for more appropriate and economically rational risk-taking.

This "sobering up" process is foundational to the private property free market system. "A private property regime makes people responsible for their own actions in the realm of material goods," wrote author Tom Bethel. "Property sets up fences, but it also surrounds it with mirrors, reflecting back on us the consequences of our own behavior. Both the prudent and the profligate will tend to experience their deserts."[xxxvii]

When we are spared from experiencing those deserts, including those that are painful, we miss important lessons and lose out on opportunities for needed reform and growth. It violates our individual self-ownership, which our nation's Founders believed was one of the self-evident truths. (Think of the Prodigal Son in Jesus' parable, who finally came to his senses and got his life on a constructive path only after others declined to bail him out.)[xxxviii] The same principle holds true for companies, economies or even nations.

Insulated from the consequences of its own behavior, Wall Street ratcheted up its risk machine, applying extreme leverage to a range of transactions and peddling exotic high-margin mortgage instruments. The financial industry and its creditors believed (correctly, as it turned out) that when the music stopped, governments would have no choice but to bail them out or risk worldwide systemic failure.

When it worked, they got to pocket the profits. When it didn't, the losses would be "socialized"; i.e., extreme catastrophic outcomes would be borne by the taxpayers. As Bank of England Governor Mervyn King candidly admitted in a 2009 speech, banks "had less incentive than others to guard against tail risk."[xxxix]

Although tail risk or chaos came to pass, government bailout funds and an implicit public backstop allowed "too big to fail" US banks to access capital on more favorable terms than other financial institutions, thereby enjoying a competitive advantage. Large banks were given a powerful reprieve in 2008—breathing room from having to boost reserves, slash leverage, or persuade investors to finance their activities by raising additional capital.

Wall Street's moral hazard–induced risk-taking appears to be alive and well in the post-bailout era. Under Dodd-Frank, the Financial Stability Oversight Council (FSOC) can designate both banks and nonbanks (such as insurance companies or hedge funds) as "systemically important." A firm whose failure could endanger the financial system would qualify as "systemically important" and be subject to additional oversight.

However, markets will rightly conclude that the government will inevitably come to the aid of any such institution. Relieved from market forces, large financial institutions no longer have to pay a cost of capital commensurate with the level of risk they are taking. These firms, in turn, again enjoy special status with creditors and are tacitly green-lighted to engage in more aggressive risk-taking.

While the FSOC is empowered to impose more stringent capital requirements on "systemically important" institutions—in theory, a powerful check on reckless conduct and an incentive for firms to avoid the designation—to have a chance of working, that type of regulatory discipline will require both substantial resolve and more transparent accounting from Wall Street. It will also require a more determined effort to stop misconduct in its tracks.

"Most wrong actions come about because people are not held accountable early enough," concluded author John C. Maxwell.[xl] There were many warning signs regarding a massive US housing bubble and a looming mortgage fiasco. Some were in the form of deteriorating market-based and economic indicators. There were also the sounds of cautionary expert voices including the likes of Barry Ritholtz, Nouriel Roubini, Chris Whalen, John Mauldin, Rick Santelli, Gary Shilling, David Rosenberg, Mike Shedlock, Michael Pento and the late Bennet Sedacca, to name just a few, who didn't simply take the "guided tour" as home prices soared.

Stop signs were missed on sovereign debt mischief as well. If the Greek government, for example, had been confronted early on about its repeated efforts to conceal the true shape of its public finances, the situation might not have proceeded on to the crisis stage. Instead, numerous warnings, including those from the International Monetary Fund, were ignored. The Greeks were permitted to run up substantially more debt by leveraging an artificially inflated credit rating to borrow at the Eurozone's cheaper financing costs. Europe's policymakers engaged in a broad pattern of denial rather than hold the Greek government accountable *early* enough, thereby allowing Greece's relatively small economy to eventually threaten the entire continent's economic stability.

The same is true of Spain, where a string of governments avoided making the hard choices about recapitalizing that country's largely insolvent banking system, each handing its successor a deeper hole. Spanish banks (aided by their domestic regulators) stubbornly avoided writing down toxic real estate assets, adequately provisioning for non-performing loans, or raising private capital. In fact, European Union officials looked the other way as Spanish banks, at the direction of their domestic regulator, the Bank of Spain, openly failed to comply with the rules established by the International Accounting Standards Boards.[xli] When Spain's current leadership finally acknowledged its banks would require at least 100 billion euros in emergency European bailout assistance, it only further subordinated the interests of private holders of both Spanish sovereign and bank debt.

While accepting the role of lender of last resort, it soon became abundantly clear that the world's political leadership shared a common strategy: Delay any politically unpopular pain or losses. As a result, the phrase "kick the can down the road" became part of the bailout era's lexicon. It is the opposite approach to earlier accountability. The strategy effectively scares off private capital due to opaque bank accounting and raises the dependency on government-sponsored subsidies and bailouts.

Designing a better financial world starts with recognition of what trust can't be based on: neither dependency nor entitlement. While the connection between actions and consequences may have been severed, trust *can* be restored to the financial system—beginning with a commitment to consistency.

Consistency of Values

"Consistency, madam, is the first of Christian duties."
— *Charlotte Bronte*

The financial world is inherently complex and subject to dynamic economic forces. As a result, flexible approaches are often required. But underlying values should never change. Remaining authentic and consistent often requires going against short-term political or performance pressures in order to preserve a better long-term system. The public will more likely support hard choices *if* they are backed by consistent values and predictable policies.

Throughout the credit crisis, many extraordinary policies were enacted under emergency powers. While expedient, some were also inconsistent, a major destroyer of trust and respect in any relationship. The inconsistencies were as damaging as some of the underlying conduct itself. Many of the pathologies of the crisis are, in fact, political in origin.

For example, policymakers refused to trust the market's reaction to ugly, but more accurate, financial statements. Before the crisis started, it was nearly impossible for even the most sophisticated of investors to glean banks' exposure to mortgage-backed securities from firms' SEC filings. When the financial house of cards began to quake, Federal

Reserve Chairman Ben Bernanke, one of the nation's leading Depression-era scholars, warned against the "pro-cyclical" or exacerbating impact of more forthright financial disclosure.

This argument, endorsed by many, rested on the notion that newly enacted fair value accounting rules and capital requirements were forcing banks to retrench and further constrict lending, thereby worsening the crisis. Supporters also claimed that former Fed chief Paul Volcker had employed similar forbearance in allowing US banks in the early 1980s to gradually work their way out of trouble by holding piles of distressed Latin American debt at face value instead of at the much lower real-time market value.

Fed officials feared that undercapitalized banks would satisfy regulatory capital requirements by dumping the bonds, securities or loans that made up their so-called risk-weighted assets. Stricter accounting rules would also require banks to sell hard-to-value illiquid toxic assets into highly distressed public markets at fire-sale prices and lead to excessive write-downs.

An aggressive post-meltdown lobbying campaign and congressional arm-twisting convinced the Financial Accounting Standards Board (FASB) to suspend a key accounting rule, FASB 157, in the summer of 2009.[xlii] Fair-value accounting mandated that banks record financial instruments at market value rather than their historical cost. Losses (or gains) are thus reflected on a company's quarterly income statement. By amending the rules, banks were required to "mark to market" only those securities they intended to sell or labeled as "fair value through profit or loss." As a result, they were given greater latitude to treat the rest of their assets differently by claiming intent to hold certain securities until repayment. Classification changes to balance sheet items thus enabled banks in both the United States and Europe to delay recognizing losses. Critics contend this approach permits financial institutions to overstate asset values.

Worried about further spooking a nervous public, regulators refused to require banks to write down toxic illiquid assets, allowing them instead to exercise "substantial judgment."[xliii] This enabled banks to retain illiquid securities at artificial book values or prices generated by internal models, rather than at current market values. Each financial institution could thus adopt a different approach to valuing the same impaired security. The Center for Audit wrote, "Valuing financial instruments absent a uniform methodology, particularly in illiquid markets, would result in inconsistent measurements and would not provide users with the most transparent or relevant information about the value of a company's financials."[xliv]

The "held for sale" versus "held for investment" distinction cries out for consistent application. Going forward, it doesn't make sense to provide banks with broad latitude between accounting buckets—that is, to capture mark-to-market prices by classifying asset prices as held for sale when they are appreciating and mark-to-model when those same assets are falling in value.

"A strong banking system should be able to survive a cyclical downturn with assets being mark-to-market in pretty much any economic environment," explained forensic accounting expert Brian Wright.[xlv] "Changing the rules in the middle of the game when things got bad for the banks probably increases the risks for another period of reckless risk taking in the future," he cautioned.[xlvi]

Because of the temporary suspension of fair value accounting, inflated assumptions about the value of real estate holdings, and the presence of complicated off-balance sheet transactions, many investors felt they could not get their arms around bank financial statements. It explains why many of the big financial institutions are still trading at a deep discount to reported book value three years later. There is an old expression, "People respect what you inspect."

Top rated bank analyst Mike Mayo claimed financial institutions were "black boxes," saying, "Every financial investor's worst nightmare is you don't know what you don't know."[xlvii] Lynn Turner, the former SEC chief economist, agreed, and hypothesized that the financial market could not heal itself because bank balance sheets could not be trusted.[xlviii] "The accounting isn't what it needs to be . . . the market is telling you that they don't believe these balance sheets in any way, fashion, shape or form," said Mr. Turner.[xlix] The opaque accounting treatment and banks' delays in recognizing losses were dubbed "extend and pretend" by critics.

"The first lesson of the financial crisis is not that the capital markets were poorly regulated or that the banks were too leveraged or that the government needed better processes for taking over failing institutions,"[l] cautions respected investigative financial journalist Jesse Eisinger. "The first lesson is that when they are in trouble, banks will mislead the world about their financials. And some will lie."[li]

In order to boost confidence, federal supervisors, including the Federal Reserve, Federal Deposit Insurance Corp., Office of the Comptroller of the Currency, and Office of Thrift Supervision, conducted a series of "stress tests" on the nation's nineteen largest financial institutions in 2009. The tests were aimed at identifying which institutions might need additional support, particularly under potentially adverse future economic scenarios. "This transparent, conservatively designed test should result in a more efficient, stronger banking system," Treasury Secretary Timothy Geithner confidently declared.[lii]

However, when the results and methodology were released to the public, many saw the tests as an obvious attempt to gloss over the banking sector's problems rather than deliver an accurate assessment of financial system risks. Most experts agreed that the tests' assumptions were not "stressful" or rigorous enough. Even "Saturday Night Live" parodied the tests with a fictional Mr. Geithner claiming, " . . . at the banks' suggestion we went with a pass-pass system."

In 2012, the Federal Reserve won wider praise for issuing revised stress tests of the same institutions' ability to withstand more dire economic stresses. Others, though, were still not satisfied with the transparency. "To this day, the Fed has disclosed little detail about how the second stress test was conducted. . . . the Fed hasn't released its estimates of banks' revenues, post-stress capital ratios or losses for asset classes, such as real estate,"[liii] wrote *ProPublica's* Jesse Eisenberg.

Financial statements weren't the only thing lacking in consistency. Sensing the public's anger, politicians were quick to launch investigations into conflicts of interest and self-dealing involving both the ratings agencies and the nation's largest banks.

At the same time, members of Congress and their staffs were themselves exempt from the nation's insider trading laws. Even though congressional oversight routinely brought elected officials into possession of non-public, market-sensitive information, they were free to trade upon the insights gleaned without owing the same duty of confidentiality. It wasn't until a CBS "60 Minutes" story exposed this self-dealing loophole in 2011that a chastened Congress quickly reintroduced legislation that had been languishing since 2006 to restrict members of Congress from trading on material non-public information.

Inconsistent behavior could be found at the other end of Pennsylvania Avenue as well. In April and again in July of 2011, the Standard & Poor's ratings agency warned that a downgrade of the US credit rating was likely forthcoming unless Washington could raise its short-term debt ceiling while also demonstrating meaningful commitment to long-term deficit reduction. President Obama, trying to force the hand of his political opponents, warned in a nationwide address that it was imperative "to avoid a credit downgrade and the higher interest rates that all Americans would have to pay as a result."[liv] Yet, when S&P followed through with the downgrade after messy political gridlock impeded progress, the administration blasted the ratings agency for its allegedly flawed methodology.

A similar "shoot the messenger" approach was employed by political leaders throughout Europe as well—criticizing ratings agencies during the financial crisis for their lack of independent ratings of mortgage derivatives, only to subsequently attack them for using their independent judgment to issue downgrades of sovereign debt, thereby putting a crimp in irresponsible Eurozone borrowing habits. Jens Weidmann, head of the Deutsche Bundesbank, offered a welcome reminder to Europe's leaders that ratings agencies are "in the end, bearers of bad news, not the originators."[lv]

Perhaps the most effective way to perceive the importance of consistency in the financial system is to try to view the world through the eyes of individual investors. Since the late 1990s, they have been subjected to a jarring series of boom-bust market cycles and ad hoc economic policies. These policies have produced two 40 percent-plus corrections in equity prices in little over a decade. As a result, small investors are naturally skittish and disillusioned. While some have unrealistic performance expectations, most would gladly trade the last decade for steady returns and consistent policy.

When the United States Federal Reserve engages in massive quantitative easing and makes credit cheaper and more available, the Fed's governors count on us to "feel" wealthier from inflated asset prices and then to act as though we are in fact wealthier. The hope is that this "wealth effect" will induce consumers, particularly the most affluent, to spend more freely on discretionary items, thereby stimulating the real economy out of its doldrums.

Not everyone trusts what the Fed is doing. "They're lying to us," says legendary investor Jim Rogers.[lvi] He believes the S&P 500's more-than-three-year rally from the March 2009 bottom is the direct result of the Fed "printing money as fast as they can."[lvii] Rogers warns that the Federal Reserve is ruining an entire class of investors: "When you destroy the class that saves and invests in your country, you are going to have serious problems down the road."[lviii]

In this regard, the Fed's zero interest rate policy (ZIRP) is misaligned with America's demographic trends and is forcing some investors outside their comfort zone. Aging baby boomers are becoming more risk-averse as they enter the stage of life when they need regular income to sustain their lifestyles. Gone are the investment clubs of the late 1990s, a byproduct of an era in which many viewed investing as a type of adventure sport. Without the "fun" of easy profits, the number of investment clubs in America has dwindled from 60,000 before the bursting of the tech bubble to roughly 5,500.[lix]

In its place, a more serious and sober environment has emerged. Some savers have remained paralyzed on the sidelines, expecting yields to rise as they normally would when the real economy recovers. With safe haven investments increasingly scarce and pinched by artificially low rates, others hunted for income farther out on the risk curve. During the first two months of 2012, for example, retail investors poured nearly $12 billion into junk-bond funds, accessing higher-yielding bonds of companies with below-investment-grade credit ratings.[lx] These inflows were more than double the amount that went into stock funds according to research firm Lipper.[lxi]

It is a truism in the investment world that investors need good information to make sound decisions, yet the Fed's frequent interventions make a hard task for investors even harder. One major problem is that the Fed's policy to suppress interest rates changes the very definition of the "risk-free" rate, a critical tool in investment analysis that historically has been tied to default-free Treasury yields. The risk-free rate is an essential component in estimating the cost of equity and capital. If the risk-free rate is converted into an artificial measure, how can the world's largest economy efficiently allocate capital, and how can the small investor know what is prudent? Comparing Treasury yields to things like the rate of inflation or the dividend yield on stocks becomes a convoluted exercise.

Historically, the bond market was seen as a barometer of the health of the US economy, pricing in expectations for economic improvement in the form of higher interest rates. But the Fed is currently pricing the bond market beyond any sense of fundamental value or economic reality. The price information from the bond market is therefore unreliable. As a result, the risks of mushrooming budget deficits are not accurately reflected in Treasury yields, and hard questions about debt sustainability are ignored while the federal government blunders on, borrowing more than 40 cents out of every dollar it spends.

Warren Buffet, the chairman of Berkshire Hathaway Inc., wrote of the low-yielding risks, "Right now bonds should come with a warning label."[lxii] That's because when rates rise, bond prices fall. Calling government bonds "among the most dangerous of assets," Buffet cautioned that inflation, fueled by cheap money and a devalued dollar, eats into purchasing power and bondholder returns.[lxiii]

While Mr. Buffet may prefer stocks to the negative real yields of government debt, the volatility of even dividend-paying stocks, popular among investors seeking income, may be too much for some to handle. Consider this: From the top in the fourth quarter of 2007 through its bottom in the first quarter of 2009, the Dow Jones US Select Dividend index lost 53.8 percent, versus a 50.2 percent loss for the S&P 500, according to Fran Kinniry, an investment strategist at Vanguard Group.[lxiv]

In a financial ecosystem trying to rebuild trust, it is important for the Federal Reserve to acknowledge the risks and costs of its policies. Low interest on savings reduces incentives to save and sparks financial volatility at precisely the wrong moment in America's demographic cycle. Since the credit crisis began, deflation has posed the greater threat than inflation. But money printing historically has led to disastrous consequences throughout the world. While the Bernanke Fed is confident that they will know when to pull the right levers, it's important that monetary authorities demonstrate respect for possible future inflationary effects and the present pain felt by America's savers trapped in a near-zero interest rate environment.

Keeping interest rates artificially low may dislodge long-term inflation expectations or crowd out private investment through the issuance of mountains of government debt. In the near term, the Fed's ZIRP/weak-dollar policy clearly contributed to stubbornly high oil and commodity prices, pushing down the standard of living for many Americans by decreasing their real purchasing power.

Investors piled into energy-related assets in 2008, in part due to attractive industry fundamentals. The oil market is truly a global market with price determined by supply and demand as well as differences in quality. But what Washington refused to admit was that the Federal Reserve's own easy-money policies were devaluing the US dollar, making crude and anything else denominated in dollars more expensive.

It is unclear whether ZIRP is capable of achieving the Fed's goal for the real economy, namely putting Americans back to work. A similar prolonged policy has failed to wake Japan from its long economic slumber. In the United States, many businesses have capitalized on Mr. Bernanke's cheap money policies to invest in productivity-enhancing technologies and machines rather than hiring new workers. As a result, low-cost credit has helped American businesses increase production through labor-saving technologies. Today the US economy is producing more goods and services than it did when the recession officially began in December 2007, but with about five million fewer workers.[lxv] From an economic perspective, these increases in productivity are positive, but the government's conscription of the capital markets to help it in the federal bailout war is impeding the natural market process of new enterprises being created to make use of workers no longer needed in earlier modes of production.

The jury is out on much of what has been done to pull the world from the depths of the Great Recession. Experimental surgery always comes with great risks. Did the policies save the financial system, as some have contended? Perhaps. Or did they simply make the imbalances larger and enable governments to remain complacent about enacting meaningful fiscal reforms?

The housing market, while appearing to have formed at least a short-term bottom in most parts of the country, has yet to demonstrate any meaningful recovery, despite record-low mortgage rates and a host of government sweeteners, such as the first-time homebuyer tax credit. Some say the interventions have artificially inflated home prices. In the words of investment manager and financial blogger Barry Ritholtz, "For a lasting recovery, we need to see houses cheap enough that they fall into "good hands"—long-term owners who can afford their mortgage payments."[lxiv] Others contend that home buyers lack urgency since the Bernanke Fed has assured them that interest rates will remain at record low levels for many years to come.

Mr. Bernanke, one of the nation's leading academic scholars on the causes of the Great Depression, steadfastly believes in applying the lessons he has drawn from that period. Bond market expert James Grant would prefer Bernanke to widen his historical view: "If Chairman Bernanke were in the room, I would respectfully ask him why this persistent harking back to the Great Depression? It is one cyclical episode, but there are many others."[lxvii] The severe Depression of 1920–21, for example, bore many similarities to the depression that followed a decade later, but the policy response was radically different and far more effective, resulting in a booming economy by late 1922.[lxviii]

Like Wall Street itself, policymakers can be prone to hubris. Limitations apply to the role of government intervention, just as they do with exotic financial innovations. There are boundaries beyond which there are diminishing, then negative, returns. For example, Jens Weidmann, president of the German Bundesbank, conceded in the late spring of 2012 that the European Central Bank's bond-buying program to save Europe's troubled banking sector had reached its "limits."[lxix] Mr. Weidmann's statement was refreshing in its unusual candor, for it almost has become taboo for central bankers around that world to admit to any limitations in their policy options. Central bankers and finance officials have preferred the image of themselves armed with a "bazooka" and an unlimited supply of policy ammunition.

Studying the post-crisis analysis, MIT economist Andrew Lo concluded, " . . . there is still significant disagreement as to what the underlying causes of the crisis were, and even less agreement as to what to do about it. But what may be more disconcerting for most economists is the fact that we can't even agree on all the facts."[lxx]

The erosion of trust within the financial system and its devastating impact is not in dispute, however. It's the one fact upon which everyone agrees. Without a new model for restoring financial trust based on consistent values, the impact of any reforms will be limited and superficial. That effort also requires leveling with the public about things that go bump in the financial night. Like Alexander Solzhenitsyn said, "One word of truth outweighs the whole world."

Notes, Chapter 6

i Nassim Nicholas Taleb, "End Bonuses for Bankers", *The New York Times*, November 7, 2011.
http://www.nytimes.com/2011/11/08/opinion/end-bonuses-for-bankers.html.

ii The Holy Bible: Mark 4:22 (NIV).

iii Tom Heneghan, "Ex-banker turned Hindu monk urges Wall Street to meditate," *Reuters*, November 17, 2011,
http://www.reuters.com/article/2011/11/17/us-protest-occupy-hindu-idUSTRE7AG0K620111117.

iv The Holy Bible: Ephesians 2:25 (NIV).

v The Holy Bible: Mathew 7:5 (NIV).

vi John C. Maxwell, "To Lead Others, First Lead Yourself," *SermonCentral.com*.
http://www.sermoncentral.com/articleb.asp?article=John-Maxwell-How-to-Lead-Yourself&ac=true.

vii Statement by William K. Black, Associate Professor of Economics and Law, University of Missouri – Kansas City, Before the Committee on Financial Services, United States House of Representatives, April 20, 2010.
http://www.house.gov/apps/list/hearing/financialsvcs_dem/black_4.20.10.pdf.

viii Keith Jurow, "How Widespread Mortgage Fraud Toppled the US Housing Market," *World Property Channel*, April 27, 2010.
http://www.worldpropertychannel.com/us-markets/residential-real-estate-1/real-estate-news-mortgage-fraud-countrywide-new-century-mortgage-afg-financial-robert-morganthau-fitch-ratings-new-york-daily-news-huffington-post-2433.php.

ix Ibid.

x Ibid.

xi Andrew Haughwout, Donghoon Lee, Joseph Tracy, and Wilbert van der Klaauw, "'Flip this House': Investor Speculation and the Housing Bubble," Federal Reserve Bank of New York, December 5, 2011.
http://libertystreeteconomics.newyorkfed.org/2011/12/flip-this-house-investor-speculation-and-the-housing-bubble.html.

xii Ibid.

xiii Ibid.

xiv Ibid.

xv Shelly Banjo and Nick Timiraos, "For the Costliest Homes, Foreclosure Comes Slowly," *The Wall Street Journal*, February 28, 2012. http://online.wsj.com/article/SB10001424052970204369404577209181305152266.html.

xvi Forrest Jones, "Sam Zell: Government Hurts Housing Recovery with Mortgage 'Moral Hazard,'" *Money News*, May 11, 2012. http://www.moneynews.com/Headline/Zell-Government-Bailout-Housing/2012/02/09/id/428898.

xvii Ibid.

xviii Robbie Whelan, "Second Mortgage Misery," *The Wall Street Journal*, June 7, 2011. http://online.wsj.com/article/SB10001424052702304906004576369844062260756.html.

xix Ibid.

xx Steffanie Marchese, "CNBC Transcript: Former Treasury Secretary of the US and Founder of the Paulson Institute, Hank Paulson Sits Down with Andrew Ross Sorkin Today on CNBC's 'Squawk Box,'"*CNBC.com*, February 15, 2012. http://www.cnbc.com/id/46252924/CNBC_EXCLUSIVE_CNBC_TRANSCRIPT_FORMER_TREASURY_SECRETARY_OF_THE_U_S_AND_FOUNDER_OF_THE_PAULSON_INSTITUTE_HANK_PAULSON_SITS_DOWN_WITH_ANDREW_ROSS_SORKIN_TODAY_ON_CNBC_S_SQUAWK_BOX.

xxi Ibid.

xxii Ibid.

xxiii President Obama's Remarks at Stock Act Bill Signing, April 4, 2012. http://www.whitehouse.gov/the-press-office/2012/04/04/remarks-president-stock-act-bill-signing.

xxiv William K. Black Interview with Bill Moyers, *PBS*, April 3, 2009. http://www.pbs.org/moyers/journal/04032009/transcript3.html.

xxv Hugh Son, "Dimon Vows Fight Moynihan Lost Over Claims from Mortgages," *Bloomberg*, April 12, 2012.

http://www.bloomberg.com/news/2012-04-12/dimon-vows-fight-moynihan-lost-over-claims-from-mortgages.html.

xxvi Sheldon Richman, "JP Morgan Lesson: End Government Bank Guarantees," *The New American*, May 18, 2012, http://www.thenewamerican.com/opinion/item/11444-jpmorgan-lesson-end-government-bank-guarantees.

xxvii Robert G. Wilmers, "Small Banks, Big Banks, Giant Differences," *Bloomberg*, June 12, 2011. http://www.bloomberg.com/news/2011-06-13/small-banks-big-banks-giant-differences-robert-g-wilmers.html.

xxviii Ibid.

xxix Ibid.

xxx Peter Eavis, " The Volcker Rule and the Goldman Controversy," *The New York Times DealBook*, March 14, 2012. http://dealbook.nytimes.com/2012/03/14/the-volcker-rule-and-the-goldman-controversy/.

xxxi "Adding Up the Government's Total Bailout Tab," *The New York Times*, July 24, 2011. http://www.nytimes.com/interactive/2009/02/04/business/20090205-bailout-totals-graphic.html.

xxxii Federal Reserve Press Release, March 20, 2012. http://www.federalreserve.gov/newsevents/press/other/20120320a.htm.

xxxiii Ron Paul speech for the National Association of Home Builders at the 29th Annual Cato Monetary Conference. http://www.youtube.com/watch?v=dEnxqZfODfs.

xxxiv Carmen M. Reinhart, "Financial Repression Back to Stay," *Bloomberg*, March 11, 2012. http://www.bloomberg.com/news/2012-03-11/financial-repression-has-come-back-to-stay-carmen-m-reinhart.html.

xxxv Simon Kennedy and Rich Miller, "Central Banks Commit to Ease as Threat of Lost Decades Rises," Bloomberg, June 25, 2012. http://www.bloomberg.com/news/2012-06-25/central-banks-commit-to-ease-as-threat-of-lost-decades-rises-1-.html.

xxxvi Susanne Walker, "Banks Buy Treasuries at Seven Times Pace in 2011," *Bloomberg*, March 12, 2012. http://www.bloomberg.com/news/2012-03-12/banks-buying-treasuries-at-seven-times-2011-pace-as-deposits-beat-lending.html.

xxxvii Tom Bethell, *The Noblest Triumph: Property and Prosperity Through the Ages* (New York: St. Martin's Press, 1998), 31.

xxxviii The Holy Bible: Luke 15: 11-24 (NIV).

xxxix Speech by Mervyn King to Scottish business organizations, Endinburgh, October 20, 2009. http://www.bankofengland.co.uk/publications/Documents/speeches/2009/speech406.pdf.

xl Maxwell, "To Lead Others, First Lead Yourself."

xli Jonathan Weil, "The EU Smiled While Spain's Banks Cooked the Books," Bloomberg, June 14, 2012. http://www.bloomberg.com/news/2012-06-14/the-eu-smiled-while-spain-s-banks-cooked-the-books.html.

xlii Ian Katz and Jesse Westrbrook, "Mark-to-Market Lobby Buoys Bank Profits 20 percent as FASB May Say Yes", *Bloomberg*, March 29, 2009. http://www.bloomberg.com/apps/news?pid=newsarchive&sid=awSxPMGzDW38.

xliii Ian Katz, "FASB Eases Fair-Value Rules Amid Lawmaker Pressure," *Bloomberg*, April 2, 2009. http://www.bloomberg.com/apps/news?pid=newsarchive&sid=agfrKseJ94jc.

xliv Center for Audit Quality, "Fair Value Accounting Fact Sheet," July 15, 2009. http://thecaq.org/newsroom/pdfs/CAQ_Fair_Value_Accounting_Fact_Sheet.pdf.

xlv Brian Wright interview with the author, April 5, 2012.

xlvi Ibid.

xlvii Mike Mayo interview with CNBC television, November 1, 2011. http://www.cnbc.com/id/45119166/Banks_Are_Challenged_I_Invest_Elsewhere_Leon_Cooperman.

xlviii Lynn Turner interview with CNBC television, November 1, 2011. http://video.cnbc.com/gallery/?video=3000054796.

xlix Ibid.

l Jesse Eisinger, "In Scrutiny of JP Morgan Loss, Bigger Questions Left Unanswered," *ProPublica*, May 16, 2012.
http://dealbook.nytimes.com/2012/05/16/in-scrutiny-of-jpmorgan-loss-bigger-questions-left-unanswered/.

li Ibid.

lii David Ellis, "Stress Tests: Banks need $75 billion," *CNN Money*, May 8, 2009.
http://money.cnn.com/2009/05/07/news/companies/stress_test_announcement/index.htm.

liii Jesse Eisinger, "Fed Shrugged Off Warnings, Let Banks Pay Shareholders Billions," *Pro Publica*, March 2, 2012.
http://www.propublica.org/article/fed-shrugged-off-warning-let-banks-pay-shareholders-billions.

liv Address by President Barack Obama to the Nation, July 25, 2011.
http://www.whitehouse.gov/the-press-office/2011/07/25/address-president-nation.

lv Todd Buell, "ECB Weidmann, Unlimited Bond Buys Not in Line with EU Treaty," *Dow Jones Newswires*, April 5, 2012.
http://blogs.wsj.com/economics/2012/01/18/ecbs-weidmann-unlimited-bond-buys-not-in-line-with-eu-treaty/.

lvi Jeff Macke, "Fed is 'Ruining an Entire Class of Investors' Says Jim Rogers," *Yahoo Finance*, December 6, 2011.
http://webcache.googleusercontent.com/search?q=cache:xwSOSdGLVagJ:finance.yahoo.com/blogs/breakout/fed-ruining-entire-class-investors-says-jim-rogers-153315477.html+Jeff+Macke,+percentE2 percent80 percent9CFed+is+ percentE2 percent80 percent98Ruining+an+Entire+Class+of+Investors percentE2 percent80 percent99+Says+Jim+Rogers, percentE2 percent80 percent9D+Yahoo+Finance,+December+6,+2011&cd=1&hl=en&ct=clnk&gl=us.

lvii Ibid.

lviii Ibid.

lix Chris Taylor, "Tight budget, wild markets hurt investment clubs," *Reuters*, December 12, 2011.
http://www.reuters.com/article/2011/12/12/us-usa-investing-clubs-idUSTRE7BB19M20111212.

lx Matt Wirz, "Buyers Take a Shine to 'Junk,'" *The Wall Street Journal*, February 27, 2012. http://online.wsj.com/article/SB1000142405297020383300457724721335 7570048.html.

lxi Ibid.

lxii Warren Buffet, "Why stocks beat gold and bonds," *Fortune*, February 9, 2012. http://finance.fortune.cnn.com/2012/02/09/warren-buffett-berkshire-shareholder-letter/.

lxiii Ibid.

lxiv Jason Zweig, "The Dangers of Dividend Funds," *Smart Money*, April 12, 2012. http://www.smartmoney.com/invest/mutual-funds/the-dangers-of-dividend-funds-1334181617214/.

lxv Catherine Rampell, "Reasons Abound for Ebb in Job Growth," *The New York Times*, May 4, 2012. http://www.nytimes.com/2012/05/05/business/economy/us-added-only-115000-jobs-in-april-rate-is-8-1.html?pagewanted=all.

lxvi Barry Ritholtz, "Spring brings signs of hope and renewal – except in the housing market," *The Big Picture*, April 14, 2012. http://www.ritholtz.com/blog/2012/04/spring-brings-signs-of-hope-and-renewal-except-in-the-housing-market/.

lxvii James Grant, "Piece of my mind," *Grant's Interest Rate Observer*, March 23, 2012. http://www.grantspub.com/userfiles/files/g30n06d.pdf.

lxviii Mark W. Hendrickson, "Yo-Yo Economics?", www.forbes.com, April 26, 2012; Mark W. Hendrickson, "We Could Use a Man Like Warren Harding Again," *Center for Vision and Values*, Aug. 12, 2009. http://www.visionandvalues.org/2009/08/we-could-use-a-man-like-warren-harding-again/.

lxix Ambrose-Evans Pritchard, "George Soros and the Bundesbank's Patriotic Putsch," *The Telegraph*, April 19, 2012. http://blogs.telegraph.co.uk/finance/ambroseevans-pritchard/100016361/george-soros-and-the-bundesbanks-patriotic-putsch/.

lxx Andrew W. Lo, "Reading About the Financial Crisis: A 21-Book Review," Prepared for the *Journal of Economic* Literature, January 9, 2012. http://www.argentumlux.org/documents/JEL_6.pdf.

7 Block Party

Lasting financial reform depends upon improving interpersonal relations. The only way trust can be restored is to get Wall Street and its neighbors talking (and listening) again. However, many on the right want only unregulated capitalism while the left is only interested in more government solutions. A new, more constructive engagement model for the financial industry requires a shift in the way Wall Street faces the world—less intellectual pride, more transparency, more awareness—*as well as* a shift in the way the world faces Wall Street. Genuine engagement involves 360-degree accountability.

That healing starts with the financial community valuing the voice of Occupy Wall Street and others like it. Clearly Occupy Wall Street has shaped the debate and given voice to the public's frustration. Federal Judge Robert P. Patterson referenced the influence of the Occupy Wall Street movement when handing down his insider trading sentence for former hedge fund manager Drew K. Brownstein. "They're complaining about the money, what they consider greed,"[i] the judge said of the protestors. "And I think that most people agree with that."[ii] Legendary bond investor Bill Gross told Bloomberg Television, "To not have sympathy with Main Street as opposed to Wall Street is to have blinders."[iii]

Some on Wall Street, however, would like to simply forget the near-death experiences of the banking system. Despite the discomfort, the industry can benefit from self-analysis and accountability. It's time to take the blinders off; there is much to be learned.

The same is true for policymakers. When asked if he saw a critically-acclaimed HBO movie about the 2008 crisis based on the Andrew Ross Sorkin book "Too Big to Fail," Fed Chairman Bernanke replied, "I saw the original."[iv] But just as Wall Street must reexamine its own behavior, so, too, Mr. Bernanke and the political class in Washington should reflect on their own actions and the extent to which they contributed to or exacerbated the crisis. None of the stakeholders should close themselves off from the rich and growing treasury of human insight and experience.

It is equally important for protest movements, whether the Tea Party on the right or Occupy Wall Street on the left or smaller bands of populist reformers, to constructively engage the institutions of capitalism. Dylan Pahman of the Acton Institute, a think tank dedicated to promoting free market policies based on Judeo-Christian morality writes, " . . . is it just to assume that all wealthy people have gotten there by unjust means? Is it right to put all the blame for our country's economic woes on these people, labeling ourselves the 'ninety-nine righteous who have no need of repentance' (Luke 15:7)? Indeed, prejudice against 'the 1 percent' will only make matters worse."[v]

Social movements also have a duty to more fully understand the challenges faced by financial institutions if they seek to be effective advocates for economic justice and garner more widespread support. "It's all ad hoc, more poetry slam than platform. Too bad it's not serious in its substance,"[vi] wrote *The Wall Street Journal's* Peggy Noonan. Harvard economics professor and Mitt Romney advisor Gregory Mankiw observed in an op-ed entitled *"Know What You're Protesting,"* "I applaud the protesters for thinking beyond their own parochial concerns and trying to make society a better place for everyone. But my second reaction was sadness at how poorly informed the Harvard protesters seemed to be."[vii] He continued, "As with much of the Occupy movement across the country, their complaints seemed to me to be a grab bag of anti-establishment platitudes without much hard-headed analysis or clear policy prescriptions."[viii]

Some in the Occupy Wall Street movement, however, recognized the need for a serious articulation of a more concrete reform agenda. A series of open source wiki pages working groups popped up at various Occupy camps, trying to lay out an unofficial framework of agreed-upon grievances, such as campaign finance reform and restoration of the Glass-Steagall Act. An offshoot group called "Occupy the SEC" drafted a thoughtful and detailed 325-page policy statement.[ix]

By sending the document to regulators, the group demonstrated that elements of the movement could meaningfully contribute to the substantive regulatory reform process, working to change the system with a high degree of sophistication.

Religious leaders have an important role to play in crafting financial reform as well, including bringing financial professionals into the discussion in an attempt to bridge differences and find common ground. The leadership of lower Manhattan's Trinity Wall Street Episcopal Church, for example, maintained a running, open dialogue with the Occupy Wall Street protesters encamped in Zuccotti Park, a square of open space just north of the church itself. The church also provided indoor space for the occupiers.

Many in the religious community have been supportive of the Occupy Wall Street movement and its self-described "peaceful witness against economic injustice." Well-known pastor Jim Wallis praised the Occupy Wall Street Movement: "Our faith communities and organizations should swing their doors wide and greet the Occupiers with open arms, offering them a feast to say 'thank you' for having the courage to raise the very religious and biblical issue of growing inequality in our society."[x]

However, political scientist Dr. Paul Kengor identifies the need to hold the movement *itself* accountable and takes exception to the reluctance of some religious leaders to call out the bad actors in the Occupy movement who have engaged in theft, destruction of property, drug use and sexual assaults.[xi] The Occupy encampments have also forced cash-strapped cities across the country to shoulder heavy police, overtime, trash removal and park repair costs, in addition to disrupting many local small businesses.

Wall Street certainly deserved a harsh wakeup call—a glass of cold water in the face. A constructive long-term dialogue, however, requires a more respectful tone. "A gentle answer turns away wrath, but a harsh word stirs up anger."[xii] Executives have increasingly felt the need to defend their success, taking particular exception to sweeping generalizations. The Acton Institute's Dylan Pahlman contended, "By crying out against 'the 1 percent,' many good-intentioned people are unintentionally dehumanizing the 'tax collectors' of our day, not all of whom are actually to blame and half of whom are in the business of wealth and job creation: entrepreneurship."[xiii] Occupy activists themselves insist that the unlawful acts of a small number of protestors should not obscure the legitimate grievances of the larger peaceful movement. Fair enough, but shouldn't a similar standard apply toward Wall Street's substantial core of "good stewards?"

Some feel that the White House itself has aggravated the problem of tone. Leon Cooperman, the chairman of hedge fund Omega Advisors Inc. and a Goldman Sachs alumnus, penned a heavily circulated open letter to President Barak Obama. Cooperman's letter resonated with many in the business community who feel increasingly isolated and singled out for harsh criticism. In it, he took the president to task for encouraging class divisions: "What does matter is that the divisive, polarizing tone of your rhetoric is cleaving a widening gulf, at this point as much visceral as philosophical, between the downtrodden and those best positioned to help them."[xiv]

Cooperman and others are deeply frustrated by what they believe is a lack of acknowledgement for life struggles that preceded their own economic success. "My father was a plumber who practiced his trade in the South Bronx after he and my mother emigrated from Poland. I was the first member of my family to earn a college degree. I benefited from both a good public education system (P.S. 75, Morris High School and Hunter College, all in the Bronx) and my parents' constant prodding. When I joined Goldman Sachs following graduation from Columbia University's business school, I had no money in the bank, a negative net worth, a National Defense Education Act student loan to repay, and a six-month-old child (not to mention his mother, my wife of now 47 years) to support."[xv]

"It's really hard to build a business," Brad Anderson, the former CEO and vice chairman of Best Buy, told Fox News' John Stossel.[xvi] Anderson, a pastor's son who dropped out of seminary, explained that many in the media and government don't have an appreciation for the difficulty of achieving success in the challenging world of business.[xvii] Former South Dakota Senator George McGovern, who opened a bed and breakfast upon leaving office, conceded, "I wish that during my years in public office I had firsthand experience about the difficulties business people face."[xviii] Anderson said he once told a group of pastors, "One of the biggest surprises I had was that acting in your own self-interest can build a more moral environment."[xix]

The American dream rests on the notion that capitalism rewards hard work and ambition. According to one recent study, just 40 percent of Americans attribute higher incomes primarily to luck rather than hard work—compared with 54 percent of Germans, 66 percent of Danes, and 75 percent of Brazilians.[xx] Mr. Cooperman emphasizes that thrift, industry, sacrifice, risk and often failure tend to accompany great success. This is a familiar refrain from wealthy Americans who are anxious to remind the so-called "99 percent" that in many cases, they were one of them—and often not very long ago.

Treasury Secretary Timothy Geithner, for example, himself a Dartmouth graduate, frequently referred to the wealthiest Americans as "the most fortunate among us."[xxi] Mr. Geithner's intentional use of the word "fortunate," implying to some a reference to "luck," echoes similar sentiment expressed by former senator John Edwards, in both his television ads in Iowa during the Democratic primary and again in his 2004 vice presidential debate with Dick Cheney. Edwards painted a picture of the wealthy, who "sitting by their swimming pool, collecting their statements to see how much money they're making, make their money from dividends, [and] pay a lower tax rate than the men and women who are receiving paychecks for serving on the ground in Iraq."[xxii]

This thinking ignores the fact that millions of retired Americans rely on the steady stream of income produced by dividends or that corporations already paid taxes on dividends to investors out of after-tax profits. For example, 70 percent of all taxpayers who received dividends in 1998 earned less than $68,000 in income, with median wages of just over $55,000[xxiii]—hardly the profile of the idle rich.

Cooperman claims he sympathizes with the protestors at some level and has been advocating adding a 10 percent tax surcharge on all incomes over $500,000 for the next three years.[xxiv] "You'll get more out of me" (meaning engagement), Cooperman said, "if you treat me with respect."[xxv]

Mr. Cooperman and his wife have taken the "giving pledge," committing to give the majority of their wealth to philanthropy. Other banking, investment, and venture capital titans (and spouses) who have also taken the pledge include Bill Ackman, John Arnold, Michael

Bloomberg, Warren Buffet, Ray Dalio, John Doerr, Glen Dubin, Ken Langone, Carl Icahn, Irwin Jacobs, Vinod Khosla, Ronald Perelman, Pete Peterson, Julian Robertson, David Rubenstein, Herb Sandler, Thomas Secunda, Jim Simons and Sanford Weil.[xxvi]

There are numerous examples of Wall Street philanthropy, ranging from Houston energy trader John Arnold's support of the Innocence Project that helps exonerate wrongly accused death row inmates to quantitative guru Jim Simons' $25 million gift to Stony Brook University, where he once served as chair of the mathematics department. Some of Wall Street's most generous donors rarely grant media interviews and do not actively seek recognition for their gifts.

Others emphasize the importance of the voluntary nature of giving. "There are people in need of help. Charity is one of the nobler human motivations,"[xxvii] wrote conservative scholar Dr. Walter Williams. "The act of reaching into one's own pockets to help a fellow man in need is praiseworthy and laudable. Reaching into someone else's pocket is despicable and worthy of condemnation."[xxviii]

Home Depot cofounder Kenneth Langone told Brandeis University students, "People who share their time and treasure don't need to be put on a pedestal, but don't vilify them."[xxix] He added that his father taught him that charity meant giving that involved sacrifice, doing without something in order to make the gift.[xxx]

"We are supposed to admire success,"[xxxi] Mr. Cooperman told Bloomberg News. Indeed, if financial success comes from serving the needs and wants of others, it would be perverse not to admire it. This is not a "gospel of wealth" argument. Jesus taught that material wealth is not a proxy for spiritual worthiness or acceptability to God. He clearly taught that those who "trust in riches"[xxxii] have a hard time finding spiritual riches—the invaluable things that can't be bought.

It seems that the Preacher in the book of Proverbs has found the happy medium: " . . . give me neither riches nor poverty."[xxxiii] That sounds rather middle-class, doesn't it? Yet, that verse can also pose a special dilemma in today's world: If one delivers economic value to large numbers of people (doing good to one's neighbor multiplied by thousands or millions), then one is liable to become rich. We certainly don't want to place limits on how much good anyone can do for others, do we?

Charity designed to relieve suffering and lift the burden of poverty off the backs of the poor is part of the Judeo-Christian ethos. We concur with the Talmudic message, "The noblest charity is to prevent a man from accepting charity; and the best alms are to show and enable a man to dispense with alms."[xxxiv] In the modern world, we most effectively achieve this goal by finding ways for invested capital to put people to work producing goods and services of value to others, thereby enabling them to support themselves by their own efforts.

Let us never forget: The antidote for poverty is wealth. Poverty is a miserable condition, an age-old curse afflicting the human race. The World Bank estimates that rising food prices pushed an additional 44 million people into poverty between June 2010 and January 2011.[xxxv] The only way to combat this tragic wretchedness is to expand the sphere of wealth production.

The good news is that our ability to create wealth has multiplied in the last few centuries to such an extent that for the first time in human history, high standards of living are widespread. One by one, societies are discovering that profit-seeking enterprises, when free from oppressive government controls, can transform an economically undeveloped society into an affluent society.

Having wealth is neither good nor bad in and of itself. It is how one becomes wealthy that matters. Wealth can represent virtue or vice. It can result from giving value to others—loving one's neighbor in a practical way—or by being harmful and taking value from others.

The Scripture says, "You cannot serve God and Money."[xxxvi] If people acquire wealth in ways that are harmful or unfair to their fellow man, whether by crime (theft, fraud, cheating, etc.) or in a way that is legal (obtaining special favors through the political process—what economists call "rent seeking"), then they are guilty of serving money, a "taker." If, on the other hand, their prosperity flows out from having rendered good and righteous service to one's fellow man, then one is loving his neighbor, a productive economic "maker."

We have the choice to do good for others or to do ill. Capitalism and freedom enable us to make this choice. We all share the same block. So let us choose wisely.

Notes, Chapter 7

i Peter Lattman, "Ex-Fund Manager Gets Prison Term in Insider
  Trading Case," *The New York Times DealBook*, January 11, 2012.
  http://dealbook.nytimes.com/2012/01/11/ex-fund-manager-gets-
  prison-term-in-insider-case/?nl=business&emc=dlbka32.

ii Ibid.

iii Linette Lopez and Robert Johnson, "You Won't Believe What Bill
  Gross And Larry Fink Said About Occupy Wall Street On
  Bloomberg," *Business Insider*, November 22, 2011.
  http://www.businessinsider.com/bill-gross-and-larry-fink-on-
  occupy-wall-street-2011-11#ixzz1mhKkwoZE.

iv John Hilsenrath and Nick Timiraos, "Bernanke Joins Bargain
  Hunters Who Refinance," *The Wall Street Journal*, December 13,
  2011.
  http://online.wsj.com/article/SB1000142405297020433610457709
  4700478530784.html.

v Dylan Pahman, "Occupy Wall Street: Shunning the Lost Sheep,"
  Acton Institute, November 30, 2011.
  http://www.acton.org/pub/commentary/2011/11/30/occupy-wall-
  street-shunning-lost-sheep.

vi Peggy Noonan, "The Divider vs the Thinker," *The Wall Street
  Journal*, October 29, 2011.
  http://online.wsj.com/article/SB1000142405297020355410457700
  2262150454258.html.

vii Gregory Mankiw, "Know What You're Protesting," *The New York
  Times*, December 3, 2011.
  http://www.nytimes.com/2011/12/04/business/know-what-youre-
  protesting-economic-
  view.html?_r=2&ref=business&nl=business&emc=dlbka21.

viii Ibid.

ix Occupy The S.E.C. Comment Letter, January 13, 2012.
  http://www.scribd.com/doc/81484886/Occupy-the-SEC-
  Comment-Letter-on-the-Volcker-Rule.

x Jim Wallis, "A Church Sanctuary for the Occupy Movement," *Huff
  Post Religion*, November 17, 2011.

http://www.huffingtonpost.com/jim-wallis/a-church-sanctuary-for-th_b_1099377.html.

xi Paul G. Kengor, "In 1920, US saw the carnage of class warfare," *The USA Today*, November 8, 2011. http://www.usatoday.com/news/opinion/forum/story/2011-11-08/occupy-wall-street-bombing/51125358/1.

xii The Holy Bible, Proverbs 15:1, (NIV).

xiii Pahman, "Occupy Wall Street: Shunning the Lost Sheep," November 30, 2011.

xiv Andrew Ross Sorkin, "It's Tone, Not Taxes, a Tycoon Tells the President," *The New York Times DealBook*, December 5, 2011. http://dealbook.nytimes.com/2011/12/05/a-rich-mans-grievance-with-obama/.

xv Ibid.

xvi Brad Anderson Interview with John Stossel, *Fox News*, December 9, 2011. http://www.youtube.com/watch?v=lQqjsLC_cQ8; http://www.youtube.com/watch?v=L5zYkjet8Zs.

xvii Ibid.

xviii Ibid.

xix Ibid.

xx Luigi Zingales, "Who Killed Horatio Alger," *City Journal*, Autumn 2011. http://city-journal.org/2011/21_4_meritocracy.html.

xxi "Geithner says the top 1 percent have a tax rate in the low 20s," *Tampa Bay Times Political Fact Check*, July 12, 2011. http://www.politifact.com/truth-o-meter/statements/2011/jul/12/timothy-geithner/geithner-says-top-1-percent-have-tax-rate-low-20s/.

xxii Transcript: Vice Presidential Debate, October 5, 2004. http://www.washingtonpost.com/wp-srv/politics/debatereferee/debate_1005.html.

xxiii Norbert Michel, Ph.D., "Who Really Benefits from Dividend Tax Relief," *The Heritage Foundation*, January 7, 2003. http://www.heritage.org/research/reports/2003/01/who-really-benefits-from-dividend-tax-relief.

xxiv Ross Sorkin, "It's Tone, Not Taxes, a Tycoon Tells the President," December 5, 2011.

xxv Max Abelson, "Bankers Join Billionaires to Debunk 'Imbecile' Attack on Top 1 percent," *Bloomberg*, December 19, 2011. http://www.bloomberg.com/news/2011-12-20/bankers-join-billionaires-to-debunk-imbecile-attack-on-top-1-.html?reflink=FINS_mcf_20111221.

xxvi The Giving Pledge. http://givingpledge.org/#enter.

xxvii Walter E. Williams' Quotes. http://www.quotationcollection.com/author/Walter_E._Williams/quotes.

xxviii Ibid.

xxix David Nathan, "Business man says it is better to give than to receive," *Brandeis Now*, April 24, 2012. http://www.brandeis.edu/now/2012/april/cohenlecture.html.

xxx Ibid.

xxxi Abelson, "Bankers Join Billionaires to Debunk 'Imbecile' Attack on Top 1 percent," December 19, 2011.

xxxii The Holy Bible: Mark 10:24 (KJV).

xxxiii The Holy Bible: Proverbs 30:8 (NIV).

xxxiv Quoted in F.A. Harper, "The Greatest Economic Charity," in *The Writings of F.A. Harper*, vol. 2, Institute for Humane Studies, 1979, p. 564, quoting a paraphrase by Mary Baker Eddy from Moses Maimonides in his *Code of Jewish Law*, Chapter X, para. 7. http://mises.org/daily/3879#note1.

xxxv The Millennium Project, "Global Challenges Facing Humanity." http://www.millennium-project.org/millennium/Global_Challenges/chall-03.html.

xxxvi The Holy Bible: Mathew 6:24 (NIV).

8 A Full House

Financial reform isn't just about looking back. It's also about preparing to rise up to meet the challenges of the future. Two challenging tests soon lie ahead. Each will require Wall Street to operate with great efficiency and integrity. Both are also unique opportunities for Wall Street to redeem itself.

An unprecedented bumper crop of motivated, talented entrepreneurs will soon be seeking startup capital, financing, and advisory and investment banking services. Growth companies require multiple access points to capital. Therefore, entrepreneurs need the capital markets to remain perpetually "open for business," and the American educational system to produce a steady stream of world-class workers. Secondly, the first baby boomer turned 65 on January 1 of 2011, starting a demographic snowball rolling down a very large hill. The traditional retirement safety net will be tested like never before.

Therefore, a wave of young entrepreneurs and aging baby boomers will soon be on Wall Street's doorstep. Both will need a financial system operating at the top of its game, accompanied by sound monetary and fiscal policy. Neither generation can afford boom-and-bust ethics or economics.

A Bumper Crop of Entrepreneurs

According to the Kauffman Foundation, 54 percent of the nation's 18–34-year-olds ("Millennials") want to start a business—if they have not already done so.[i] Sixty-four percent of Latinos, 63 percent of African Americans, and 45 percent of white young adult Americans indicate such a desire.[ii] A recent Gallup Poll also found that nearly eight in ten students (77 percent) in grades five through twelve say they want to be their own boss, 45 percent say they plan to start their own business, and 42 percent say they will invent something that changes the world.[iii] Carl Schramm, president of the Kauffman Foundation, says these polls reveal "a generation that is enthusiastic about entrepreneurship, and that is good news for the United States. They recognize that entrepreneurship is the key to reviving the economy."[iv]

With plummeting computer hardware and data storage costs, the advent of cloud computing, open-source software, voice technologies, the iPhone and Android development platforms, and the proliferation of outsourced service provider solutions, powerful "agile" innovations, and "lean" startups can come to market with incredible speed. Business schools also continue to develop entrepreneurship curriculums with more than 2,000 college and universities in the United States, about two-thirds of the total, now offering courses in entrepreneurship, compared to just sixteen in 1970.[v] The Global Consortium of Entrepreneurship Centers (GCEC) includes two hundred university members, many of which provide essential mentoring, coaching and resources to entrepreneurs and small businesses within their communities.

How the financial sector meets entrepreneurial demand will go a long way to determining American global competitiveness. China, for example, was forced to dramatically tighten credit during 2010–11 in an attempt to cool off its runaway property market and high food prices. The Chinese attributed the inflationary pressures, in part, to Federal Reserve Chairman Ben Bernanke's easy money policies. While generally effective at letting some of the air out of the property market, Beijing also inadvertently cut off the credit lifeline to its small business sector, forcing many firms to turn to usurious black market lenders. The problem prompted Prime Minister Wen Jiabao to instruct regulators and tax collectors to lighten up on banks that lend to small businesses and instructed them to promote special economic zones to support hi-tech firms.[vi]

The Chinese are rushing to erect an innovation framework with breakneck speed, trying to outrun building wage pressures by moving up the production value chain. The stated goal of the nation's long-term strategic plan is to become an innovation-oriented country by 2020.[vii] This is evidenced by the fact that China accounted for 12.3 percent of the world's total R&D spending in 2010, second only to the United States.[viii] China's 279,298 patent applications in 2009 also trailed only the United States.[ix]

In the United States, the financial system, not planners in Beijing, delivers capital to startup innovators through a variety of mechanisms, including loans, venture capital and private equity infusions. Other funding sources, such as credit cards, friends and families, and angel investors, can also play an important role. Later, Wall Street supports their growth through IPOs, secondary offerings and debt issuance. When the financial crisis erupted, many small, newly formed and startup companies experienced a severe shortage of funding options. Funding became dear, forcing many entrepreneurs to give up considerable equity to secure financing.

There is some evidence that the painful experience of the crisis years is still affecting the way capital is being raised among fledgling companies. Firms are taking on larger capital infusions, in part to build up war chests in the event financing seizes up again. The new-venture–tracking website, Techcrunch reports, "The overall trend is no surprise to anyone who has been following tech investing in the last several years—companies are now raising "seed" and "angel" rounds that are nearly as big as Series A rounds."[x]

Research shows banks also play a surprisingly important role in advancing new ventures. In a 2009 paper entitled "The Capital Structure Decisions of New Firms," authors Alicia Robb and David T. Robinson conclude, "Contrary to many accounts of startup activity, the firms in our data rely heavily on external debt sources such as bank financing, and less extensively on friends and family-based funding sources. This fact is robust to numerous controls for credit quality, industry, and business owner characteristics."[xi]

Robb and Robinson offer this important cautionary finding: "The heavy reliance on external debt underscores the importance of well-functioning credit markets for the success of nascent business activity."[xii] When credit markets became frozen, banks dramatically reduced their exposure to the so-called "cash flow-based" small business loan market.

Lending suffered another body blow during the crisis when CIT Group Inc., an important New York-based lender to small and mid-size businesses, filed for bankruptcy in November 2009.[xiii] While it did not garner the media attention of the Lehman Brothers bankruptcy, the CIT bankruptcy had a profound impact on certain segments of the small business market. Although conditions have clearly improved since the depths of the crisis and CIT Group ultimately emerged from bankruptcy, the environment for middle-market lending remains challenging.

In response to a stubbornly sluggish economic recovery, politicians offered a variety of measures to enhance access to capital and the availability of credit for small and startup businesses. Many of these provisions enjoyed broad bipartisan support. They included proposals to expand the seed-funding pool beyond sophisticated, so-called "accredited" individual investors and also enable small startup companies to raise capital through crowdfunding, a primarily online technique that allows individual investors to pool their money.

Ultimately, Congress settled on the Jumpstart Our Business Startups Act (JOBS Act) in the spring of 2012, aimed at loosening the prohibitions on general solicitation and crowdfunding by small businesses. The goals of the act, including democratization of the capital raising process, are noble.

However, most white-collar criminal and securities law experts expressed serious reservations about the JOBS Act. Ordinary mom-and-pop investors are drawn to the opportunity to get in on the ground floor of the next Google or Apple. But liquidity and reporting are both extremely limited for outside investors in private companies, raising concerns about suitability for small, unsophisticated investors. Heath Abshure, the Arkansas securities commissioner, told *The Economist* in reference to similar earlier proposals, "I am terrified," warning against a "wild, wild west" market.[xiv]

Provisions of the JOBS Act are intended to make it easier for companies to go public. In truth, most companies that want to go public have had little difficulty in accessing the public markets under *normal* market conditions. The answer is not to water down disclosure regulations, underwriter research restrictions, or investor protections. Public companies should be subject to a serious vetting process, and underwriter conflicts of interest have proven to be real. Instead, the answer is to ensure that the funding markets never completely freeze up again as they did during the financial crisis. Bubbles, fueled by dishonest financial conduct and unconstrained credit, are ultimately the entrepreneur's worst enemy.

Entrepreneurs also require ready access to high-skill workers, human capital to invent the future. Once again, a stable and fair market system has an important role to play in funding the necessary educational infrastructure. Moody's economist Mark Zandi says, "Our greatest gem is our educational institutions. It is going to take 100 years for anyone, anywhere on the planet to replicate what we've got there."[xv]

Educational competitiveness is critically important as jobs inevitably follow brainpower and advanced skills. Applications from China, for example, now comprise nearly half of all international applications to US graduate programs.[xvi] As an increasing number of colleges and universities bring significant portions of their curriculum online, it will further provide important job retraining skills and lifelong learning opportunities. According to the 2011 Survey of Online Learning, the number of students taking at least one online course has now surpassed six million, or 31 percent of higher education students.[xvii]

With fewer state and federal dollars available across the educational spectrum, however, Wall Street will be asked to lead the way in scaling America's higher education advantage. Numerous colleges and authorities (which can issue bonds on behalf of nonprofit organizations such as universities) have tapped the bond market to borrow money. For example, Dartmouth College announced in 2009 that it planned to sell $400 million in bonds to fund campus construction projects.[xviii] Harvard was also able to issue $2.5 billion in bonds at the height of the financial crisis in 2008, providing much-needed liquidity to the venerable institution.[xix]

Beyond the ability to borrow, endowment success is also incredibly important to college scholarships and research. These funds benefit from the power of compounding. US News reports that the average private college endowment in 2009 was $296,479,664 among the 754 private colleges that disclosed their figures.[xx] Nearly three-quarters of colleges and universities peg their endowment spending at about 5 percent of a three-year rolling average of total endowment market value. During 2010, college and university endowments posted a national average rate of return of 11.9 percent, rebounding nicely from several difficult years of performance.[xxi]

Notre Dame, for example, represents best practices among college endowment funds. Led by Vice President and Chief Investment Officer Scott Malpass, Notre Dame's roughly $7 billion endowment, a third of which is devoted to scholarship funds, has averaged a 12.1 percent return over a fifteen-year time period.[xxii] Notre Dame was the only one of the twenty largest university endowments that did not have to cut endowment spending as a result of the 2008 financial crisis.[xxiii]

Notre Dame and other influential endowments are also increasingly playing an important role in keeping elite investment managers honest in their fees. Rather than accept hedge funds' traditional 2 percent management fee and 20 percent annual incentive fee, Notre Dame links fees to longer-term performance criteria. This sophisticated market-based activism, in turn, forces asset managers to refine their own investment process to include a greater emphasis on a company's long-term cultural and corporate governance issues. Recognizing the importance for financial professionals to consider larger impacts, Mr. Malpass proudly points out that Notre Dame has taught ethics in its business school since 1978.[xxiv]

Malpass and his colleagues embrace a long-term investment horizon, willing to wait for more illiquid and more global investments to produce. Relying upon a fund of funds (or multi-manager) endowment approach, Notre Dame allocates roughly 30 percent of its endowment to hedge funds and another 30 percent to private equity managers.[xxv]

Private equity investor Jay Jordan, who chairs the Notre Dame Board of Trustees Investment Committee, explained to CNBC television in the fall of 2011 how important it is for Wall Street professionals to personally experience the impact of their labor.[xxvi] "We have our investment managers out for a [football] game every year and big dinner. We all thank them,"[xxvii] recounted Mr. Jordan. "I tell them, 'As you walk around campus tomorrow, you will run into many students, many of whom are on financial aid and are here because of the great work that you, our managers, do for them.' We take that very seriously. Financial aid is a key component."[xxviii] Restoring the bond between Wall Street professionals and their ultimate clients' well-being is a powerful tool for making a better financial world.

Boomer Moment

Much like endowments support essential scholarships, pension and retirement funds comprise one of the pillars of social stability. The financial crisis exposed serious structural cracks in the global public and private pension systems, however. At the same time, the intensity of demographic demands is accelerating, producing a very narrow margin for future financial missteps.

Among the 34 Organisation for Economic Co-operation and Development (OECD) countries, there were seven people of working age for every one of pension age in 1950.[xxix] Today the number is around four to one.[xxx] The OECD estimates that by 2050, there will be fewer than two people of working age for every one aged over 65 on average across member countries.[xxxi]

The relationship between Wall Street and retiree quality of life will be obvious. Retirees will be selling stocks and other retirement assets to fund living expenses. At the same time, boomers will be consuming more, pushing up goods prices and creating even greater demand for income.

These realties make it imperative that we develop policies that help us avoid the excesses of boom-bust economic cycles. Private pension funds around the world, for example, lost 23 percent of their value in 2008, worth $5.4 trillion.[xxxii] The OECD also clarifies the impact beyond investment returns: "Earnings are under pressure from wage cuts and shorter working hours. This reduces revenues from pension contributions and increases the demand for unemployment and other benefits."[xxxiii]

A pension scheme's assets relative to its ability to pay current and future liabilities is referred to as its "funding ratio." The global asset/liability ratio is well below 1998 levels. In Ireland, the United Kingdom and the United States, funding ratios for defined-benefit plans have fallen from 110-120 percent to around 75 percent.[xxxiv] It is now quite common for a pension fund to be 25 percent underfunded, whereas in the 1990s they were 100 percent funded, says Roger Urwin, global head of investment content at human resource consulting firm Towers Watson.[xxxv]

In the United States, the Pension Benefit Guaranty Corporation guarantees the defined benefit pensions of about 44 million US workers, stepping in to backstop a company's pension plan when a firm goes belly up and walks away from its obligations.[xxxvi] *The Financial Times* reports that the PBGC currently pays about $460 million a month to support roughly 870,000 retirees.[xxxvii] The system is financed by levies or premiums on healthy US firms that also offer defined-benefit pension plans. However, the gap between the PBGC's assets and its obligations has ballooned to $26 billion.[xxxviii] While the plan is to raise premiums to help fund the shortfall, the US taxpayer is ultimately on the hook.

Abnormally high stock market volatility brought on by rolling financial crises on both sides of the Atlantic has damaged investor psychology. The United Kingdom, the world's third-largest pension market, has the greatest allocation exposure to equities, 55 percent (although that is down from 74 percent in 2000). United States, Australian and Canadian pension funds also tilt more heavily toward equities than the rest of the world.[xxxix] At the end of 2010, the average global asset allocation of the seven largest markets was 47 percent equities, 33 percent bonds, 1 percent cash and 19 percent other assets.[xl]

In the United States, nearly 45 percent of 55–65-year-olds held more than 70 percent of their private pension assets in equities, according to the Employee Benefit Research Institute.[xli] Tired of the whipsaw action and approaching retirement, respected investment strategist David Rosenberg has been predicting that both American households and pension funds would increasingly rebalance their asset allocations toward greater fixed-income allocations.[xlii]

Mr. Rosenberg writes, "So maybe Ma and Pa Kettle are moving to correct this mismatch on their balance sheet and adjusting it to capture more income, limit their risks and preserve their capital. We do know with certainty that the median age of the baby boom cohort is approaching 55. As strategists we have to come to the understanding that a powerful demographic trend is gathering momentum, which is generating this insatiable appetite for yield—an era of correcting the underweight in bonds in the aging (but not aged) boomer asset mix while correcting the lingering overweight in equities."[xliii]

Pension funds will similarly continue to boost their bond exposure, says Rosenberg.[xliv] However, both are likely to be negatively impacted by the US Federal Reserve's current zero interest rate policy. Fed Chairman Ben Bernanke has promised to keep nominal rates artificially low for an extended period (at least until 2014). While these policies favor borrowers, they come at the expense of savers and further compound pension funding problems. Rosenberg warns, "The dramatic decline in the 30-year bond yield is going to aggravate already-massively actuarially underfunded positions in pension funds."[xlv] Low rates push up the present value of future pension payments, increasing a fund's liabilities. Pension fund managers are also tempted to take on more risk in order to enhance lagging returns.

Demographic headwinds are indeed formidable. Pension reforms will require strong leadership and broadly shared sacrifice. The financial crisis has already accelerated the shift from defined-benefit to defined-contribution plans. But within defined-benefit plans, difficult adjustments will be needed, and those changes will leave policymakers scrambling to avoid reducing benefits in a way that would further injure troubled economies.

In the coming years, the demands on the financial system will be considerably greater and the margin for error much slimmer. Entrepreneurial job creators will need steady access to capital. So will companies seeking to expand into high growth international markets. University endowments and pension/retirement funds will also require stable growth and maintenance. There are few issues of greater national importance than reforming the behavior and borrowing habits that produce financial bubbles. Neither dismantling nor indulging Wall Street will cut it this time. The house will soon be very full. "When you enter a house, first say, 'Peace to this house.'"[xlvi]

Notes, Chapter 8

i Kauffman Foundation Press Release, "An Entrepreneurial Generation of 18- to 34-Year-Olds Wants to Start Companies When Economy Rebounds, According to New Poll," November 10, 2011. http://www.kauffman.org/newsroom/millennials-want-to-start-companies-when-economy-rebounds-poll-says.aspx.

ii Ibid.

iii Valerie J. Calderson, "US Students Entrepreneurial Energy Waiting to be Tapped," *Gallup*, October 13, 2011. http://www.gallup.com/poll/150077/Students-Entrepreneurial-Energy-Waiting-Tapped.aspx?utm_source=alert&utm_medium=email&utm_campaign=syndication&utm_content=morelink&utm_term=Entrepreneurship percent20-.

iv 2011 Young Invincibles Policy Brief, *Kauffman Foundation*. http://www.younginvincibles.org/News/Releases/YI_PolicyBrief_Kauffman_2011.pdf.

v Judith Cone, "Teaching Entrepreneurship in Colleges and Universities: How (and Why) a New Academic Field Is Being Built," *The Ewing Marion Kauffman Foundation*, http://www.kauffman.org/entrepreneurship/teaching-entrepreneurship-in-colleges.aspx.

vi "Fearful Symmetry," *The Economist*, November 19, 2011. http://www.economist.com/node/21538790.

vii Karin Wall, "Richard Li-Hua on Innovation in China," *Innovation Management*, November 23, 2011. http://www.innovationmanagement.se/2011/11/23/richard-li-hua-on-innovation-in-china/.

viii Ibid.

ix David Barboza, "China Poised to Lead the World in Patent Filings," *The New York Times Economix*, October 6, 2010. http://economix.blogs.nytimes.com/2010/10/06/china-poised-to-lead-world-in-patent-filings/.

x Eric Eldon, "Crunch Base Reveals: The Largest Seed and Angel Fundings From the Past Thirty Days," *TechCrunch*, November 21, 2011.

http://techcrunch.com/2011/11/21/allyourcrunchbasearebelongto
us/?utm_source=feedburner&utm_medium=feed&utm_campaign
=Feed percent3A+techcrunch percent2Ffundings-exits+
percent28TechCrunch+ percentC2 percentBB+Fundings+
percent26+Exits percent29.
xi Alicia Robb and David T. Robinson, "The Capital Structure
Decisions of New Firms," February 11, 2009.
http://papers.ssrn.com/sol3/papers.cfm?abstract_id=1345895.
xii Ibid.
xiii Andrew R. Johnson, "CIT's Thain sees opportunity to gain share,"
MarketWatch, November 16, 2011.
http://www.marketwatch.com/story/cits-thain-sees-opportunity-
to-gain-share-2011-11-16.
xiv "Many Scrappy Returns," *The Economist*, November 19, 2011.
http://mobilemarketingcn.com/magzine/economist/The.Economi
st.-.2011-11-19.=ECO.PDF.TEAM=.pdf.
xv Dave Cook, "Moody's economist Zandy sees US economic
positives amid gloom," *The Christian Science Monitor*, July 18,
2011.
http://www.csmonitor.com/USA/Politics/monitor_breakfast/2011
/0718/Moody-s-economist-Zandi-sees-US-economic-positives-
amid-gloom.
xvi Melissa Korn, "Chinese Applicants Flood US Graduate Schools,"
The Wall Street Journal, April 3, 2012.
http://online.wsj.com/article/SB100014240527023047504045773
19922446665462.html.
xvii "Going the Distance: Online Education in the United States,
2011," *The Sloan Consortium*.
http://sloanconsortium.org/publications/survey/going_distance_2
011.
xviii Mitch Davis, "College to issue over $400 million in bonds," *The
Dartmouth*, May 26, 2009.
http://thedartmouth.com/2009/05/26/news/bonds.
xix Zoe A. Y. Weinberg, "University Bond Sale Raises Less Than
Expected," *The Harvard Crimson*, November 12, 2010.
http://www.thecrimson.com/article/2010/11/12/harvard-
university-bonds-bond/.

xx Katy Hopkins, "10 Private Universities with Largest Financial Endowments," *US News*, June 28, 2011. http://www.usnews.com/education/best-colleges/articles/2011/06/28/10-universities-with-largest-financial-endowments.

xxi "Investment Returns Averaged 11.9 percent in FY 2010," *2010 NACUBO-Commonfund Study of Endowments*, January 27, 2011. http://www.commonfund.org/InvestorResources/CommonfundNews/Documents/2011 percent200127 percent202010 percent20NCSE percent20Full percent20Data percent20Press percent20Release.pdf.

xxii Scott Malpass and Jay Jordan interview with CNBC Television, October 31, 2011. http://video.cnbc.com/gallery/?video=3000054478.

xxiii Ibid.

xxiv Ibid.

xxv Ibid.

xxvi Ibid.

xxvii Ibid.

xxviii Ibid.

xxix OECD, "Pensions and the Crisis," *Pensions at a Glance 2009: Retirement Income Systems in OECD Countries*, 2009. http://www.oecd.org/dataoecd/10/26/43060101.pdf.

xxx Ibid.

xxxi Ibid.

xxxii Ibid.

xxxiii Ibid.

xxxiv Julia Kollewe and Phillip Inman, "Value of global pension funds hits record high at £16tn, study shows," *The Guardian*, February 7, 2011. http://www.execreview.com/2011/02/value-of-global-pension-funds-hits-record-high-at-16tn-study-shows/.

xxxv Ibid.

xxxvi Jeremy Lemer, "US faces pension bill for AMR restructure," *The Financial Times*, November 30, 2011. http://www.ft.com/intl/cms/s/0/ae535ad4-1b67-11e1-8b11-00144feabdc0.html#axzz1uhDYCBk5.

xxxvii Ibid.

xxxviii Ibid.

xxxix "Global Pension Asset Study 2011," *Towers Watson*, February 2011. http://www.towerswatson.com/assets/pdf/3761/Global-Pensions-Asset-Study-2011.pdf.

xl Ibid.

xli OECD, "Pensions and the Crisis," 2009.

xlii Joe Weisenthal, "David Rosenberg Delivers Long, Must-Read Rebuttal of the 'Bond Bubble' Talk," *Business Insider*, August 19, 2010. http://articles.businessinsider.com/2010-08-19/markets/30063457_1_treasury-bonds-bond-funds-equities#ixzz1exlq0e2a.

xliii Ibid.

xliv Ibid.

xlv Tyler Durden, "Rosenberg Presents The Three Ways Bernanke Disappointed The Market, And Why It Is Dumping," *Zero Hedge*, September 22, 2011. http://www.zerohedge.com/news/rosenberg-presents-three-ways-bernanke-disappointed-market-and-why-it-dumping.

xlvi The Holy Bible: Luke 10:5 (NIV).

9 A House with a Story

Every house has a story, memories made by both current and prior occupants. If America's prior "owners" strolled by one summer afternoon, would we invite the elderly couple inside? After all, we share a special bond. Would we leave a note for the next owners? If so, what would it say?

Such a heart-to-heart talk would be timely now that our financial system is at a crossroads. The memories of the financial crisis have started to fade in the minds of some on Wall Street. The risk is that as the financial world slowly adjusts to a new post-crisis "normal," Wall Street's leadership reimports the same broken and polarizing value system. And if it turns out that the relative calm of the past few years has merely been the eye of the financial hurricane and nothing fundamental has changed, then we're really in trouble.

If the Great Recession taught us anything, it is that the financial system is so interconnected and so essential to our daily lives that Wall Street's business decisions can no longer be ignored and be regarded as private matters, but are of great public concern to us all. Financial professionals are now part of the mosaic that forms the public trust, along with the likes of police, fire, educators, elected officials, healthcare providers and clergy.

With that responsibility, it's important for Wall Street not to forget the things it once knew. That starts with a sense of national purpose. There are very few symbols that can communicate America's grand potential like Wall Street. Whoever wins the next presidential election should deliver a speech in lower Manhattan in which he challenges Wall Street to, in effect, "put a man on the moon by the end of the decade. Your country needs you." That does not mean a goal of Dow 30,000, but rather a goal of a vibrant economy, with vigorous growth of existing and new businesses, correspondingly abundant job opportunities, and rising standards of living across the board—in other words, a thriving capitalism in which the American Dream is alive and well.

Challenging Wall Street to do better is a joyful goal, not a burden. It is good to bless people through more wealth creation—more products, more services, more jobs, more achievement, more satisfaction, etc. As hard as it may be for some to believe, Wall Street remains a very patriotic community, and the financial world can be mobilized to promote the national good. In the days after the attack on Pearl Harbor, for example, the Treasury asked investment bankers and companies to refrain from using corporate bonds so as not to compete with the federal government's suddenly expanded needs.[i] At the same time, though, Wall Street should not be seen as the handmaiden of government, relied upon by Washington to perpetually finance dysfunctional government and runaway spending. When World War II ended, government issues of war bonds trailed off dramatically and new stock issues soon doubled.[ii]

Financial stability demands that Wall Street function as a capital "maker" rather than "taker." But Wall Street can't do this alone. Government needs to mend its ways, too. Crony capitalism—the counterfeit of the real deal—relies on special government favors to secure wealth. Crony or fiat capital, also counterfeit, makes crony capitalism possible through the unconstrained expansion of credit based on the shaky foundation of fiat currency.

Crony capitalism and fiat credit are the two great destabilizers of the financial system. They are inherently dishonest and defraud the public, falsifying the all-important price signals that entrepreneurs and investors need to make sound financial decisions. For example, short-term interest rates currently hover around 1 percent, an artificially low rate by historical standards. What "signal" should the average investor, homeowner or small business owner glean from perpetually low interest rates? This rate implies that capital is abundant when, in fact, major banks and sovereign governments alike have been receiving bailouts fashioned out of fiat credit on a massive scale.

Interest rates are so low not because capital is abundant, but because its supply has been inflated by central bank magic while demand from the private sector has been stifled by various policies.[iii] Central bank creation of fiat money and credit necessarily causes malinvestment and makes it more difficult for market participants to hedge against systemic risks.

Those expansionary policies generate the boom-bust cycle that is often so enjoyable in the boom stage while so painful when the inevitable bust follows. When the collapse inevitably occurs, many people cry out for the government to "do something" about such jarring economic instability, not realizing that increased government deficit spending and the central bank credit creation that enables it were contributors to the instability in the first place.

As we have explored, financial repression in the private sector, accompanied by the creation of more fiat money and credit creation, has historically been the unsavory province of corrupt Third World regimes. Today, though, it seems that any profligate, deeply indebted government finds the temptation to resort to these techniques irresistible. Each cleanup effort during a post-boom bust becomes an opportunity for government to present itself as the cavalry riding to the rescue—a tactic that always ends up encroaching on the financial sector's independence. Politicians and monetary authorities increasingly exploit their domestic financial institutions as tools to ration capital, with the government itself having priority access in order to finance ever-more deficit spending.

We should never forget that the fifth point in Marx's ten-point platform for how to socialize an economy[iv] called for government to gain a monopoly on the issuance of credit. References to Marx may seem passé or inflammatory, but our house's prior owners remind us that not too long ago they once shared the block with some pretty rough neighbors.

The reality is, there comes a point where some level of debt paints any corporation or government into a corner from which it cannot naturally escape. In Greece, Ireland, Spain, Portugal, Italy and Japan, it is getting harder for each successive government to step over the drying paint.

Fortunately, the size and strength of the US economy provide some time and options to "right the ship." But there is no more mistaking the diminishing returns to debt. On the eve of the meltdown, in the summer of 2008, the Federal Reserve's "Flow of Funds" Z.1 data showed that debt in the US had become much less productive over the years. In 1960, each dollar of new debt generated 64 cents of GDP growth, whereas in 2008, a dollar only generated 15 cents of growth.[v] The law of diminishing returns had set in with a vengeance. Significantly, the official federal debt at the time those figures were published in 2008 was $9.4 trillion. Today it is nearly $16 trillion, and clearly, all that additional debt has been impotent in its attempt to generate vigorous growth.

There are two potential checks on this kind of policymaking. The first is obvious—the voters. However, elections around the world have demonstrated that voters increasingly gravitate to candidates who promise them the least amount of pain. Robbing from Peter to pay Paul consistently garners Paul's support. So does pushing the burden on to future generations by increasing federal debt.

The second check is an independent financial market that ultimately pushes back against governments that issue unacceptable, untrustworthy amounts of marketable debt. This is the classic "bond vigilante" scenario, where bond buyers demand higher coupons for the greater risk of a future restructuring event or diminished purchasing power. It is impossible to know where the fiscal cliff lies, but bondholders are the one constituency constantly keeping an eye out for that ledge. The challenge is that the influence of the private institutional bondholder is being increasingly marginalized by "uneconomic" buyers, central bank purchasers who buy US debt without regard to price.[vi] Today, only 23 percent of Treasuries are held in private hands—down from 55 percent in 1982.[vii] Artificially-low interest rates encourage foreign firms to borrow in US dollars—forcing foreign central banks to then buy dollar-denominated assets like US Treasuries to prevent local currency appreciation and maintain export competitiveness.

Acknowledging limits is the central issue, and especially the limits of human ability. Hubris poses the single greatest risk to the financial system and is the root cause of many its problems. It was hubris—overconfidence in the ability of central economic planning—that led to the costly, disastrous experimentation with socialism in the previous century. In the United States today, the stakes have gone up with the creation of "blank check" hubris, a dangerous mutation whereby both Wall Street and monetary authorities are emboldened by unlimited government guarantees. Under this thinking, no strategy appears too novel or too risky. In fact, throwing things at the wall to find out what sticks can seem downright enterprising, innovative and proactive. This assumes, however, that the process of experimentation is both costless and harmless. There are boundaries to perpetual experimentation—a clear distinction between Dr. Salk and Dr. Frankenstein.

There is a reciprocal nature to free markets: One achieves one's self-interested goal of prosperity by working hard for others (that is, *voluntarily* working hard, as opposed to working under the orders of a political authority). We can never disregard self-interest; it is ubiquitous, universal.

The beauty of the free markets is the principle that nobody may lawfully violate the freedom of another to pursue self-interest (the pursuit of happiness) and advance one's goals. Everyone's rights must be safe, protected and honored in order for justice to reign. We accept self-interested behavior as a given in human beings, but for the sake of society, we must also respect our neighbors' rights as much as we wish our own rights to be respected. The freedom to pursue self-interest ends at any point where it would violate someone else's rights. On a one-to-one basis, it is relatively easy to see how the principle of rights plays out.

Today, though, through Wall Street's creation of derivatives whose notional value equals many times the entire country's annual GDP, we need to start pondering a question that the human race has never had to confront before: In a world in which a private firm's natural right to seek profits should be sacrosanct, does any firm have the right to engage in creative financial engineering that places the entire country and world at risk if something unforeseen goes wrong? We came very close to finding out what economic devastation on an apocalyptic scale looks like just a few years ago. Perhaps, before going to—if not beyond—the brink the next time, we should ask whether freedom means the right to jeopardize the economy on which all human beings depend.

Conservatives and libertarians in the Tea Party movement as well as the Occupy Wall Street movement both saw the bailout of too-big-to-fail banks and corporations as unjust. Such intervention is not a facet of genuine capitalism. In a truly free-market capitalist system, the government never usurps the prerogative of the sovereign consumer— that is, everyone—to give the "thumbs up" or "thumbs down" signal to all businesses, based on whether the business is meeting the consumers' needs ably and at an acceptable price.

The beauty and fairness of capitalism is that people prosper in proportion to the economic value they supply to others. Indeed, what system of interpersonal economic relations could there be that would establish stronger incentives to do unto others as you would have them do unto you, and thus promote peaceful cooperation and social harmony, than a system in which the only *legitimate* way to enrich oneself is to do something of value for others? Individuals engage in voluntary exchange when both perceive themselves better off than the alternatives. It is a positive sum game.

During the depths of the financial crisis, author and columnist Peggy Noonan wrote, "So maybe wisdom begins there for them, and for those entering and living out lives in business in America: Look only to yourself and wind up with ashes. Know it's bigger than you and wind up a hero."[viii]

Acknowledging limits and respecting the property rights of others also mean harnessing society's self-interest. Always opting for more spending today rather than a better tomorrow for our children is no different than CEOs who commit accounting fraud with the knowledge that their successors will be left to deal with the fallout. When government always projects future revenues based upon the best-case scenario, it is no different than CEOs who artificially inflate today's stock price through rosy guidance.

Intergenerational theft is immoral. Debt is a tax on the economy's future growth, lowering real wages and living standards. After one generation, a 1 percentage point difference in growth rate becomes a 25 percent difference in per-capita income.[ix] Therefore, the time to save for a rainy day is when the sun is shining. Or as Joseph advised Pharaoh: to store up food during the seven good years in preparation for the seven lean years to come.[x] The next generation relies on a stable and independent financial system to act as guardian of its future, as well.

In order to be seen as part of a virtuous solution, Wall Street will need to aim high in its standards for leadership and conduct. Stand on principle. Make a culture of service, honesty and humility a strategic priority and embed it in every culture-shaping institution available. Former Treasury Secretary and Alcoa CEO Paul O'Neill summed up the state of affairs in corporate America: "Every company I know says somewhere in its annual report, 'People are our most important resource,' but my observation from all these places I had worked was that there no evidence it was true."[xi]

While regulation may serve as a powerful deterrent, it is least effective at governing interpersonal relationships. In the classic movie *Wall Street*, the master of the Wall Street universe Gordon Gekko tells his aspiring young protégé Bud Fox, "If you need a friend, get a dog." No, Wall Street needs friends who share the same values and who aren't afraid to tell each other when they are wrong or getting too full of themselves. That's what friends do—not dogs that know no wrong, sycophants that see no wrong, nor regulators who prosecute wrongdoing after the fact.

In such a harried world, there is a place for simple and timeless virtues that bind us together, notions of morality and humanity that include a sense that there is something greater than amassing money for money's sake. We need Judeo-Christian principles that have wisdom for the modern world, business school frameworks that emphasize ethical decision-making, community service opportunities that reinforce our connections to each other, or simply workplace programs that promote a better life-work balance. We say, "Create a space for all of them." A stewardship ethic draws great strength from religious, spiritual, familial, community or common sense influences. In the end, government regulation is *not* the dominant culture-shaping institution.

Over sixty years ago, William F. Buckley Jr. concluded that he would not hazard a specific formula to address Yale's perceived ills. Mr. Buckley ended *God and Man at Yale* with the following aim: "Far wiser and more experienced men can train their minds to such problems. I should feel satisfied if they feel impelled to do so, and I should be confident that job would be well done."[xii]

In the same tradition, we are not so presumptuous as to claim all the answers to Wall Street's troubles. Ultimately, the responsibility to govern Wall Street falls on the shoulders of the men and women of the financial industry. Many "far wiser" individuals have already trained their minds on financial regulatory reform.

We are also confident that if similar energy is devoted to establishing an ethical upright Wall Street culture, a more stable, independent and vibrant financial system will surely emerge. Our optimistic view stems from the simple fact that, in the words of economist Walter Williams, Americans have never done the wrong thing for a long time.[xiii] There is no reason to believe they will start now. In fact, we contend that many in the financial industry never wavered in their commitment to do the right thing and are enthusiastically awaiting principled leadership.

After nearly five years of finger-pointing and social tension, now is the time for broader and more urgent solutions. "Deep calls to deep,"[xiv] as the Psalm so eloquently states. It is time for Wall Street to grow in wisdom and stature, rather simply burnishing tarnished brands until public pressure fades with the next bull market. A financial awakening is needed—one that sees the challenge as not only placing right limits on Wall Street but also unlocking its powerful potential for goodness.

An upright financial system is an invitation to a better world. Better days and better ways. There is "a time to scatter stones and a time to gather them, a time to embrace and a time to refrain."[xv] This is the time to gather, not to scatter.